GLOBAL CIVILIZATION

GLOBAL CIVILIZATION

A Buddhist-Islamic Dialogue

By

Daisaku Ikeda and Majid Tehranian

British Academic Press
LONDON • NEW YORK

Reprinted twice in 2004 by British Academic Press
6 Salem Road, London W2 4BU
175 Fifth Avenue, New York NY 10010
www.ibtauris.com

In the United States and Canada distributed by Palgrave Macmillan, a division of
St. Martin's Press
175 Fifth Avenue, New York NY 10010

First published in 2003 by British Academic Press

ISBN 1 86064 810 X

A full CIP record for this book is available from the British Library
A full CIP record for this book is available from the Library of Congress

Library of Congress catalog card: available

Typeset in Baskerville 11/12 pt by Q3 Bookwork
Printed and bound in Great Britain by MPG Books Ltd, Bodmin

Contents

Foreword

Islam and Buddhism in dialogue? Of all the religions, these two seem the farthest apart despite over a thousand years of shared history. In recent years, some collaboration has emerged in Southeast Asia, but Muslim-Buddhist dialogue has still remained the last frontier, the least likely arena, for fruitful interfaith dialogue.

But this apparent gulf is now bridged. In a bold and imaginative act, Daisaku Ikeda, the president of Soka Gakkai International (SGI), a lay Buddhist group begun in Japan, created the Toda Institute for Global Peace and Policy Research and appointed Majid Tehranian as its founding director in 1996. This was unprecedented since Majid not only is not a member of the SGI, he is not even a Buddhist, but is a Sufi Muslim from Iran/Persia. This initiative in appointing Majid Tehranian as the director of the SGI Toda Peace Institute demonstrated in one clear stroke Ikeda's faith that what Buddhists and Muslims share in common is much more powerful than what divides them, and that people of good will must work together and be enriched by their diversity, not fearful of it, if we are to build landscapes of peace.

Earlier in the 1990s Samuel Huntington had become the center of foreign policy debate by proposing that "clashes of civilizations are the greatest threat to world peace". Huntington is less well known for also asserting the flip side of this claim, namely, that "an international order based on civilization is the surest safeguard against world war". In keeping with this vision, the United Nations decided to begin the new millennium by dedicating the year 2001 to a "dialogue of civilizations" to build a culture of peace. But in order to dialogue, civilizations need to be embodied in gifted individuals.

This present dialogue between Majid Tehranian and Daisaku Ikeda functions at many levels. Their brilliant display of cross-civilizational learning reveals a remarkable range of common ground between Buddhist and Muslim worlds. But their dialogue also reveals the passion of two visionary leaders who take us beyond the details of personal practice and the walls of their traditions to construct broad avenues for a future world without war. Both know the pain of war, and have responded since their youth with zeal to find alternatives to violence: this is a key to their dialogue. In their journeys, both have ranged across the globe to engage other activists for peace using the alchemy of dialogue to transform differences into bonds of strength.

The 20th century was by far the bloodiest and most barbaric in history as our technological advances increased our capacity to kill unrestrained by a parallel progress morally and spiritually. However, at the end of the century as the microchip was changing our globe, a historic religious development was also emerging called inter-religious dialogue. Instead of competing against each other, religious communities increasingly tried to learn from each other by using the vehicle of interfaith dialogue to explore the worlds of other religions. Beyond the excitement of discovering common ground with people of radically different religious histories, interfaith dialogue has also brought about "mutual transformation" as participants deepened and reformed their own religious practice. As a result, interfaith dialogue, especially between Christians and Buddhists, has been recognized in recent decades not only as a way to enhance one's personal religious life, but also as an important new step in human religious history. There is no better place to see the creativity and potential of interfaith dialogue than in this volume. Dialogue uses words, and Daisaku Ikeda and Majid Tehranian are skilled communicators who love words, but who love even more the meanings that go beyond words. Wilfred Smith, the former Director of the Center for the Study of World Religions at Harvard University, maintained that theology is closer to poetry than prose, and this truth is demonstrated throughout this rich volume. Majid Tehranian has inherited from the Persian poetic tradition the spiritual wings to use words to soar beyond their limits. Daisaku Ikeda is not only the inspirational leader of perhaps the most innovative Buddhist movement today, but he is also recognized as an outstanding Japanese poet. Their mutual admiration for courageous social reformers is balanced by a deep respect for the wonder and mystery of existence that challenges those who make false and oppressive claims of absolute power or truth. Their obvious delight in poetry pervades their dialogue with a joy and enthusiasm that is unique.

There have been many famous collaborations in history, but few have been more remarkable or unlikely than the teamwork of Daisaku Ikeda and Majid Tehranian in global peace work through the Toda Peace Institute. Beyond the rich tapestry that they weave from the threads of Buddhism and Islam, their dialogue expresses the inspiration and exhilaration of crossing boundaries, of discovering kindred spirits across history, and of crafting new frameworks for building cultures of peace. After testing many paths in their own journeys, their inquiring minds offer dialogue as the best sure hope for the survival and flourishing of civilization. More personally, they inspire each of us to choose dialogue within our families and neighborhoods, within our workplace and our world, as the strongest and safest road for human cooperation and peace.

Islam and Buddhism may be worlds apart doctrinally and institutionally, but in their common work of liberation, justice, and wholeness, they are two wheels for the progress of civilization. But it is the warm friendship of Majid Tehranian and Daisaku Ikeda that ignites sparks of mutual recognition across these traditions, and the pain and poetry of their lives that transforms them into two wings for the bird of peace.

David W. Chappell
Laguna Hills, CA

Preface

Dr. Majid Tehranian, on his way to visit the ruins of the Silk Road in Central Asia, stopped over in Tokyo. His stopover in July, 1992 provided our first opportunity to meet and talk.

I remember being impressed by the warm, sunny expression in his eyes. But when he began to speak of war and the problems of peace, his usually mild manner gave way to impassioned concern. I could see that I was confronting a man who harbored the true "flame of conviction" in his breast.

Both of us experienced the terrors of war in our childhoods, his in Iran, mine in Tokyo. Dr. Tehranian was born in 1937 in the Iranian city of Mashhad. Not long after, World War II broke out, and his hometown was bombed and occupied by foreign troops. As for the horrors of war, he himself has said that he "was made painfully aware that war turns people into beasts". And his youthful hatred of war and the anger it engendered in time gave way to a determination to devote his life to the creation of a peaceful world.

As a young man, Dr. Tehranian went to America and continued his studies at Harvard University, where he was active in the movement for the democratization of his native land. For this reason, when he returned later to Iran, he was immediately taken into custody at the airport. Though he was released after a short time, he remained under constant police surveillance for the following seven years.

These experiences did not deter Dr. Tehranian in the pursuit of his goal. As the proverb says, blocked waves pound that much harder. With the weight of each word one utters, one becomes a true activist in pursuit of peace, and in Dr. Tehranian's case, one who knows how to battle through the power of intellect.

In February of 1996 I founded the Toda Institute for Global Peace and Policy Research so that it could work to carry on the efforts for peace of Josei Toda, the second president of the Soka Gakkai, whose ideals are concepts I myself have long cherished: the global human family, transnationalism, and the Toda declaration against nuclear weapons. At that time I asked Dr. Tehranian to be the first director of the institute. I was impressed by his efforts to pursue studies that would benefit those who face harsh realities, and I knew he had the kind of stalwart faith needed to sustain him in the task.

Since then, Dr. Tehranian has been expanding his research network on a worldwide scale, adopting as the motto for his projects "Dialogue of Civilizations for World Citizenship", focusing on the most urgent problems of our age. In February, 2000, in commemoration of the hundredth anniversary of President Toda's birthday, an international conference on "Dialogue of Civilizations" was held in Okinawa. The Toda Institute's research work has been published in a book series on global peace and policy, including the Okinawa conference papers on a new peace agenda for a new millennium.

Dr. Tehranian is also deeply versed in the study of religion and has stressed that, in the task of mediating between one civilization and another, it is most important to have the kind of openness of heart and mind that is engendered by religion.

Dr. Tehranian, as a graduate student at Harvard, studied under Paul Tillich, one of the most outstanding theologians of the 20th century. Dr. Tillich has defined the essence of religion as "ultimate concern with the ground of being". I too believe that one must employ all the goodness inherent in human nature in a religiously motivated search for the true meaning of life; it is from the soil of that endeavor that the kind of openness of heart that comprehends the dignity of the life force will spring.

Differences of race, nationality, or culture do not of themselves create division or confrontation. It is people's hearts and minds that supply the energy that tears people apart. It is the task of religion to control the heart and mind and, while glorying in these mutual differences, to direct them towards the source from which all values are born. To fix one's eyes on the eternal, the universally valid, and in this way to bring about a revival in human values—this, it seems to me, is the prime requirement of the kind of world religion demanded by our present age.

In a religion that recognizes variety as a natural manifestation of vitality, difference will be hailed as a welcome enrichment to human society, as wisdom in its most creative and worthwhile form. In these dialogues conducted by Dr. Tehranian and myself, we have traced the spiritual sources from which flow the traditions of Shakyamuni and Muhammad, the Buddhist and Islamic traditions, and to discover how the spirit underlying them can be revived in the present. In doing so, we noted not only their points of similarity, but their differences as well, believing that in an approach that transcends both of these lies the basis for the wisdom of humanity in the time to come.

The year 2001, the gateway to the 21st century, has been designated by the United Nations as "The Year of Dialogue Among Civilizations". When we survey the long history of the human race, we see that when different civilizations came into contact with one another and deepened their relations, this in many cases led to the creation of new and important values. The historian Arnold Toynbee in his life work, *A Study of History*, has clearly illuminated this process, which he calls the dynamism of cultural encounter.

Today, though in economic terms the process of globalization is rapidly advancing, human beings feel themselves deprived of their foundations and tend increasingly to turn inward to search for their own identity. Frictions and disputes escalate alarmingly, until we fear that what we are in fact heading for is a clash of civilizations.

Are we headed for a forced uniformity imposed by a single fixed set of values, or for an uncontrolled and endless process of disintegration? Where is the thread of Ariadne that will lead us out of the Minotaur's labyrinth, as in the Greek myth, by restoring to all people a sense of the dignity of the individual and the value of life? Dr. Tehranian and I believe that the solution is to be found in the process of dialogue between one individual and another.

Dr. Tehranian, a specialist in the subject of international communication who teaches at the University of Hawaii, has succinctly pointed out the dangers confronting the present day world, "a new kind of world, a world with expanding channels of communication," in his words, but at the same time one that "is yet sorely in need of dialogue".

As he indicates, rapid technological advances such as the Internet and the other features of the much-touted IT revolution have opened up many new and highly efficient routes for the communication of data. But these do not appear to have reduced the "mind distance" that exists between individual and individual. They have not furthered the process of mutual understanding that leads to mutual trust. Too often, the data that is transmitted is stale, and received in a passive manner. And the "digital divide"—the gap between those who have access to such advanced technology and those who do not—has added to the problems.

Dr. Tehranian has given grave warning of these pitfalls that mark the information-oriented society of our time. These warnings of his that, as it were, put a finger on the sore spot, bring to mind the words of the philosopher Martin Buber. He says that real religious dialogue depends on having open minds and hearts. You must know—really see—the other party, and make the effort to appeal to him. It is an encounter between conviction and conviction, an honest exchange between character and character. If these conditions are met, then a true community will emerge. It is the spirit of such "open dialogue", I believe, that our present world is waiting for.

Now, at the turn of the century, we see signs of a desire for such dialogue even in those areas where even the longing for world peace has been a distant goal. In June, 2000, after over half a century of division, the leaders of North and South Korea for the first time began to speak directly to one another. And in July, through the mediation of America, Israel, and Palestine continued to pursue their efforts toward peace in the Middle East. In both cases, the two sides face many difficulties in attempting to reach agreement after so many years of confrontation, but at least the first step has been taken toward peaceful coexistence.

If one drop of the water of dialogue is allowed to fall upon the wasteland of intolerance, where attitudes of hatred and exclusionism have so long prevailed, there will be a possibility for trust and friendship to spring up. This, I believe, is the most trustworthy and lasting road to that goal. Therefore, I encourage the flow of dialogue not only on the political plane but also on the broader level of the populace as a whole.

In my small way, I have tried to do what I could by engaging in dialogue with intellectual leaders of the Christian, Hindu, and other religious traditions and of various cultural backgrounds, as well as with persons from countries that deny religion. My aim was to discover a road to peace through the common dimension of humanity that we all share.

It is a source of great joy to me that I have been able now to engage in these dialogues with Dr. Tehranian, an expert in the Islamic tradition that today plays such an important role in international society. I hope that our book will help to open up a "Silk Road" of the spirit linking the peoples of the world, and will provide an outlook upon which to build a new global civilization based upon mutual tolerance and harmony.

Daisaku Ikeda
Tokyo, Japan

Introduction

Choose dialogue;
For at the two crossroads of life,
Once we part,
We may never meet again.
—Hafez

Greek peripatetic philosophers knew that dialogue is the most enlightening method of learning. Socrates, Plato, and Aristotle conducted their classes while walking in the gardens of Athens. They never imprisoned themselves in the large and impersonal lecture halls of modern universities. Relations between teachers and students were direct, intimate, and personal. They questioned and were questioned. Nothing was taken for granted. Everything came under sharp scrutiny. Truth emerged in the process of conflict of ideas and perspectives through the dialectic. The conversation was open-ended. Truth was the search for the truth. No one claimed to have found it once and for all.

When I met Daisaku Ikeda for the first time in 1992 on my pilgrimage to the Silk Road, I found in him another Socrates dedicated to the art of conversation. He was extraordinarily agile both physically and intellectually. He knew me before I had met him. He put me at ease and engaged me for three hours in one of the most enjoyable conversations of my life. I learned much from him both factually and pedagogically. Our conversation, among other things, focused on the historic encounters between Buddhist and Islamic civilizations along the Silk Road. I suggested to him that maybe we should continue this conversation and turn it into a book to follow his two previous conversations with Arnold Toynbee (*Choose Life*) and Johan Galtung (*Choose Peace*). He readily agreed. We were going to call it *Choose Dialogue*.

Dialogue is a method among other methods of human communication. Other human communication methods include command (as in the military), adversarial (as in a court of law), instructional (as in a classroom), bureaucratic (as in offices), scientific (as in scientific conferences and journals), and intimate (as among friends and lovers). Each method has it own rules. Dialogue is both an end and a means to human understanding. In dialogical communication, we engage others as different but equal. We try to enter their world of meaning through an open-ended process of communication and exploration. Dialogue is premised on mutual respect and learning. In dialogue, we change through mutual appreciation, sympathy, and empathy. This is not the easiest method of human communication, but it is the most fruitful. That is why dialogue is the most meaningful path to negotiating a new global civilization based on the contributions of all past human civilizations.

The world at the dawn of the 21st century stands at a critical juncture. Accelerating global communication has brought different cultures and civilizations into direct contact in the living rooms of any home with access to radio, television, or the Internet. However, the rapidly expanding channels of global communication have not led to greater international understanding. On the contrary, the Western romance with the East, nurtured in the 18th and 19th centuries by the love of the exotic, has been largely replaced with apprehension and distaste. Commensurately, the Eastern fascination with Western scientific and technological marvels has given way to fear and loathing of Western materialism, arrogance, and militarism. At times, global terrorism has tragically supplanted global dialogue.

Paradoxically, however, Western materialism has infected the East and Eastern spiritualism has penetrated the West. A global civilization is thus in the process of formation. This book is the result of that kind of fermentation. It focuses on the spiritual and ethical foundations and contours of such a civilization when and if genuine global dialogue is pursued. It has taken us eight years, frequent meetings, and continuous correspondence to arrive at this point. We share it with you, dear reader, in the belief that something is to be gained by learning that human experience and ideas are inevitably varied around the world, but when two persons of good will enter into a sincere conversation about their own truths, a more universal truth emerges. That is what went on for thousands of years along the old Silk Road as traders and scholars from a variety of faiths—Shamanic, Zoroastrian, Hindu, Buddhist, Confucian, Jewish, Christian, and Islamic—exchanged goods and ideas. The first global economy along the Silk Road is now followed by a second global economy in the 21st century in which supersonic transportation and electronic communication are building the foundations of a new global civilization through dialogical encounters.

Ikeda has made significant contributions to the building blocs of this civilization. He is a modern master of dialogue. During the past 40 years, he has conducted over 1500 such dialogues with a rich diversity of world leaders, ranging from Linus Pauling to Chingiz Aitmatov, Rosa Parks, Henry Kissinger, and Mikhail Gorbachev. By publishing those dialogues, he has introduced millions of people to the richness of world cultures, empowered the peace movement, and enlarged global citizenship. Millions of people, members of the Soka Gakkai International and beyond, hold him high in their affection and admiration.

The structure of this dialogue naturally flows from the topics of interest to the authors. Coming as we do from two world civilizations encountering the modern humanist, scientific, and technological civilization, our worldviews reflect a complex synthesis of traditional and modern perspectives. Chapter 1 begins with a conversation on the central importance of dialogue to the physical and cultural survival of humanity in the 21st century. It moves on, in Chapters 2 and 3, to reciprocal introductions to the Islamic and Buddhist civilizations, worldviews, and cultures. Chapter 4 focuses on the encounters of Buddhism and Islam through history. These led, in the case of Islamic civilization, to the emergence and spread of a rich mystical tradition, the Sufi philosophy and poetry in Central Asia and beyond. Sufism borrows from all traditions of civility (Persian, Greek, Arab, Indian, and Chinese) to build a Gnostic worldview embedded in all great spiritual traditions. In Chapter 5, we come to a discussion on the rise of religious ecumenicalism and fundamentalism in our own times. Chapters 6–9 deal with the role of dialogue in a variety of human domains, including the cultural, educational, and political. The final two chapters focus on the contributions that dialogue can make to a world torn by political, economic, and cultural divisions and tensions.

I have learned much from a conversation that has lasted for eight years. I wish to thank those kind friends and colleagues who have supported us in this process. David Chappell, who has pioneered Buddhist-Islamic dialogue in Southeast Asia, has kindly written a foreword for this volume. Mr. Tomosaburo Hirano has persistently followed us in every step of the way by acting as a bridge between Japanese and Persian languages and cultures. Satoko Takahashi and Hau'oli Busby have given me unmatched administrative and secretarial assistance. Thanks are also due to Mr. Hiromu Yamaguchi and Ms. Celine Shinbutsu for nursing the manuscript at its final stages.

We hope, dear reader, that you also find this volume useful in your search for your own truth. We further hope that the volume advances greater international and intercultural understanding in an age of globalization, terror, and dialogue. However, we wish to encourage you to engage whoever you meet, particularly those others from foreign lands, in your own dialogic pursuit of truth.

Majid Tehranian
Honolulu, Hawaii

CHAPTER 1

Why Dialogue?

Ikeda: I have great respect for those who fight for peace. Many people talk about peace but few take action for the cause. I understand you've been to Durban in South Africa.

Tehranian: Yes, I have. The Toda Institute for Global Peace and Policy Research held an international conference there on the theme of African food security. Thank you for your thoughtful message to the conference. I'm well aware that from early on you have been very much interested in Africa, saying that the 21st century is an African century.

Ikeda: I have made every effort to meet as many African leaders as possible, including President Nelson R. Mandela of South Africa. Durban reminds me of Mahatma Gandhi ...

Tehranian: Right. Durban is the third largest city in South Africa, and that's where Gandhi's nonviolent peace movement was started. He lived there for twenty-one years from the end of the last century, organizing an anti-discrimination campaign.

Ikeda: We will be talking about Gandhi and his ideas from time to time in this dialogue, but the recent developments in India and Pakistan make me painfully aware of the need for humankind to reevaluate the concept of nonviolence and find ways to put it into practice. Nuclear warfare must be avoided at all costs.

Tehranian: I agree with you completely. It is precisely to that end that the Toda Institute has chosen "human security" as one of its principal research projects. One major subject we address is how to abolish all nuclear weapons.

I am determined not only to devote myself to research but also to build up an international network of wisdom for the ultimate abolition of nuclear weapons.

Born into a Spiritual Life

Ikeda: Before we begin our discussion, I would like to ask you about your personal background. That will help deepen our mutual understanding and it will also be a good way to introduce you to our readers.

Tehranian: Well, I was born in 1937 in an Iranian city called Mashhad. Mashhad literally means "a place of martyrdom". This is where Imam Reza, the 8th Imam of the Shi'a Islamic faith, is buried. Imam Reza came to the city in the 9th century as governor of Khorasan province, but soon after his arrival he was poisoned by his adversaries and died. He was well known as a just and righteous leader and his death was so deplored that the city was named after him as Mashhad.

Ikeda: I hear that his tomb is now a holy site to which a great many Shi'a pilgrims from all over the world come to pay tribute.

Tehranian: That's right. So, as a child, I grew up with a keen awareness of the spiritual significance of my birthplace. I now live in Hawaii, but whenever I think about my home city, the first thing that comes to mind is the golden dome of the tomb and its lofty minarets.

The dome is at the city center and I could see it from my home. We would hear the calls to prayer issuing from its minarets at sunrise, noon, and sunset.

Ikeda: The golden dome shining in the sunlight and the sounds of people's prayers vibrating throughout the town … It must have been quite a picturesque and memorable scene.

I was born in 1928 in Tokyo's Ohta ward. Of many childhood memories I remember particularly well the sight of the beautiful blue sea from the seashore near my home.

My family was in the business of gathering and processing a kind of edible seaweed called *nori*. I still have vivid memories of my father and his assistants going out to work late at night to take advantage of the rise and fall of the tide … and my mother working hard to help the family business.

Tehranian: I can never forget my mother's beautiful chanting of the Koran in the morning and at night. I'm sure that it was her voice, which I heard chanting every single day, that implanted deep religious feelings in me.

My day was punctuated by drums, *azan* chants (calls to prayer), and my mother's chants. This gave my young life a beautiful regularity, reminding me of the existence of a world beyond myself. Looking back, I think I was born into a spiritual life without knowing it.

The Folly of War: Turning People into Beasts

Ikeda: Very interesting, indeed. The peaceful days of my childhood did not last very long. When I was eleven, that horrible war—World War II—broke out.

Tehranian: I was only three, then. Despite its declared neutrality, Iran was invaded and occupied by the Allied forces. Our country was also used as a "Bridge of Victory" for transporting war materials from the Persian Gulf to a beleaguered Soviet Union.

Meanwhile, my home city Mashhad was bombarded and occupied by the Russians. While walking along the streets of the city, I remember hiding behind my mother's *chadar* so that the Russian bombs would not hit me!

Ikeda: War completely destroys the happy life of people, reduces whole towns to ashes overnight, and deprives us of the lives of our loved ones and dear friends. The horror of war is beyond imagination unless you've experienced it yourself.

Tehranian: I have one really bitter memory. One day my older brothers were swimming in the city's public pool. Some Soviet soldiers came along unexpectedly and, finding my brothers, began to bully them about. They held them under the water until they were gasping for air and would pull them out again at their whim, delighting in my brothers' desperation. They were getting their kicks from mistreating little children! I was made painfully aware that wars turn people into beasts. At times, the Russian soldiers would give us children sweets, but that sort of kind behavior was the exception, not the rule.

Wartime Experiences: Comparing Notes

Ikeda: The opening sentence of my novel *The Human Revolution* reads: "War is barbarous and inhuman. Nothing is more cruel, nothing more tragic." It was not an abstract notion, nor was it cheap sentiment, but an honest and strong expression of indignation against war, which forces everyone into tragedy.

Tehranian: That is truly moving. It wasn't until I went to school and learned reading and writing that my hatred of war led to some action. My antiwar sentiments first took a nationalist turn. In the second grade, I became a budding journalist by producing a hand-made magazine. It included stories, cartoons, and even an editorial, although quite a simple piece, to be sure!

Ikeda: What did the editorial say?

Tehranian: It focused on the Allied occupation of Iran. I used a story we had learned at school about two sisters fighting over a doll, tearing it into pieces, and leaving everyone in tears.

The accompanying cartoon showed a map of Iran being fought over by the Allied powers, the Russians in the North and the British in the South. My grandfather, who bought a copy of the magazine, said to me, "You should be censored for your own good!"

My fate was thus sealed. I became an outspoken pacifist and anti-imperialist writer for the rest of my life.

Ikeda: A crucial turning point in my life came when I was nineteen. I met Josei Toda, who was to become my mentor. I learned from him that the central pillar of the Soka Gakkai movement was Buddhism, which is pacifistic in its basic orientation. I also learned that during the Second World War, Soka Gakkai leaders fought against the militarist regime, criticizing its fanatic war effort, and as a result the founding president Tsunesaburo Makiguchi died in prison, and my mentor, too, was imprisoned. It was because of this early postwar encounter with Josei Toda that I embarked on the "road to peace" by upholding Buddhist principles.

Struggle against Authority: The True Worth of a Person

Tehranian: I myself was once taken into police custody for unjust reasons, so I can appreciate the greatness of Messrs. Makiguchi and Toda, who never compromised their convictions while in prison.

I went to the United States to study at Harvard University. There, I got involved in the movement for my country's democratization as president of the Iranian Student Association. That put me on the blacklist of the Iranian secret police.

In 1971, when I was thirty-four, I wanted to go home because I felt very homesick. My parents advised me against the plan for fear of my safety, but I decided to return anyway, partly because a friend from Harvard and a high-ranking official of the Iranian government wanted me to help him in his work.

Ikeda: That's when you were put under physical restraint.

Tehranian: Well, yes. When I arrived at Tehran, a secret police official who had been checking his blacklist file grinned as soon as he saw my passport. He must have rejoiced at catching an anti-Establishment movement leader. I was immediately taken into the security office at the airport.

As I was being taken there, I could see my family waving toward me on the other side of the glass window. They had expected me to come out soon, but when they realized what was going on, they looked really scared. They all knew well about the terror of dictatorship in Iran.

Ikeda: It sounds like a suspense scene from a movie.

Tehranian: So I asked a security official to relay a message to my family. I told them not to worry about me because I had a friend in the government who would guarantee my safety. It was just some sort of misunderstanding that I was under arrest, I said, so please go home.

The following morning I was released, as apparently the authorities were assured that I was no security risk. I nevertheless had to agree that I would report myself to the police whenever they summoned me, and that I would not leave the country without official permission. For the whole seven years I remained in Iran then, I was constantly under surveillance.

I began working soon after my return home, but I was not paid my salary at first.

Ikeda: The power of first-hand experience!

Like my predecessors Tsunesaburo Makiguchi and Josei Toda, I was put into jail on a false charge. It was July, 1957, and I was twenty-nine. I will never forget that experience.

The ruling power elite was afraid of the growing popular movement that the Soka Gakkai represented. They wanted to nip it in the bud, so to speak, before it was too late. That's why they arrested me under a false accusation, but I never yielded to any coercion or oppression by the ruling authorities.

Tehranian: I always feel great respect and admiration for the first three presidents of the Soka Gakkai for their courageous actions and uncompromising commitment to their beliefs and principles.

They each had to overcome tremendous personal suffering, and yet they all went beyond personal concerns to act for the benefit of humankind. There are many people in the world who are suffering, but it is rare to find people like yourself and your predecessors who transformed themselves to fight for a noble cause in the interest of humanity.

The Human Revolution: Source of Value Creation

Ikeda: "Transcend your personal worries and sufferings and transform yourself in such a way as to contribute your due share to society and humanity"—this is the motto of the SGI movement aimed at human revolution.

Tehranian: That's where I find the name Soka, or "value-creation", particularly significant. Take Mahatma Gandhi or Martin Luther King—people who opened a new path for creation in history. They were invariably born and lived in an era when established values were in crisis.

In order to live fully in an age of crisis and make "wisdom for creation" of new values shine forth, one must cultivate strong will-power and self-discipline so as to be able to cope with all adversity. Generally, the better disciplined a person is, the more likely he/she will challenge the established authority and open up a new path of creation in the course of struggle against the old.

Ikeda: A path of value creation in an age of crisis requires well-tempered self-discipline— I could not agree more with the point you have just made.

Professor Nur Yalman of Harvard told me that he believes "sustained challenge is the fountain of great value creation". As I interpret it, "sustained challenge" means that each man and woman must hone his or her wisdom to build up a network of solidarity among awakened people. Peace, for example, will remain an empty dream unless people have an ability to check any reckless moves of the power elite; the tragedy of war will never cease unless people unite to prevent it.

The Toda Institute—Motives and Aspirations

Tehranian: Globalization makes our world increasingly interdependent. Regrettably though, the capacity to hold a "global perspective" is still underdeveloped. I know well that you have been a pioneer in global-scale thinking and action.

Ikeda: I founded the Toda Institute for Global Peace and Policy Research in February, 1996 in the hope that it would become a focal point of efforts to grope for and formulate a new vision for the world in the third millennium. And we asked you, Dr. Tehranian, to head the Institute.

Tehranian: When I received your kind offer, I immediately knew that it would give me a rare opportunity to work with a group of peace-loving people for a cause in which I deeply believe.

I had studied the Soka Gakkai and had reached the conclusion that it is a tenacious organization in pursuit of world peace.

Ikeda: Once, in reference to the history of Soka Gakkai, you said something to the effect that founding president Makiguchi fought against the established religious authority in the name of religious reform, struggled against the military regime in the name of peace, and died a martyr for his beliefs. You found in Makiguchi the supreme model of "value creator".

So I knew you had a profound understanding of what we stand for when I asked you to direct the new institute.

Tehranian: Assuming the directorship of the Toda Institute was, for me, a "challenge to responsibility".

As we discussed the mission of the Institute with the Board of Directors, it became clear to us that we must become "a new kind of institute for a new kind of world". By "a new kind of world", I mean a world endowed with expanding channels of communication yet sorely in need of dialogue.

That is why we chose "Dialogue of Civilizations for World Citizenship" as the motto for the Toda Institute.

About the Title

Ikeda: As I recall it, you wanted to entitle this volume "Choose Dialogue" when we first talked about it.

Tehranian: Your two previous dialogues with two distinguished scholars, Arnold Toynbee and Johan Galtung, are titled *"Choose Life"* and *"Choose Peace"*, respectively. They both focused on how to preserve the sanctity of life through the pursuit of peace by peaceful means.

Those topics are problems as old as humanity itself, yet they remain of primary importance today. But we have now entered a stage of history during which "dialogue" is becoming as necessary as "life" and "peace". In fact, dialogue may be the only means by which we can guarantee life and peace.

Ikeda: After all, the proof that human beings are human lies in the spirit of dialogue. The great Persian poet Sa'adi wrote in the 13th century, "Man is superior to the beast by being able to talk, but if you do not talk about good things, the beast will be superior."

Tehranian: Globalization of markets and societies has brought different nations, cultures, and civilizations into intimate contact with each other on a massive scale. These contacts, on the other hand, have led to both competitive and cooperative economic and political formations, clashes in perceptions and interests, as well as conversations and negotiations. To the extent that dialogue is absent in such contacts, as under conditions of violence and domination, the seeds of animosity will be sown for years, even decades, to come.

Ikeda: I suppose it is against the backdrop of such a situation that some scholars like Professor Samuel Huntington of Harvard have presented the "clash of civilizations" and other similar theses.

In my view, it is not only incorrect to assume a clash is inevitable but even dangerous because such a thesis might encourage fixation on the confrontational picture of the world. Even if a clash should occur, civilizations themselves are not to blame, for the true cause lies in the kind of barbarism that does not accept groups of people that are different from one's own.

In order to prevent such a clash from taking place, we cannot emphasize too much the importance of the spirit of dialogue. For genuine dialogue requires an ultimate trust in the goodness people are endowed with and an effort to strike the right chord in their minds.

Tehranian: If dialogue is chosen as a method of dealing with our friends and foes, there is hope that we can better understand them and thereby the possibility of mutual accommodation of perceptions and interests.

Ikeda: Dialogue is the weapon of peace, and that is the fundamental spirit of Buddhism.

The Indian society of Shakyamuni's time was, in a way, similar to the present-day world as it was in the period of transition and change. Values were in utter confusion, and various contending forces were engaged in violent struggles for power and influence.

Even at home, it is said, people had to have their weapons close at hand. Such social unrest notwithstanding, Shakyamuni literally traversed the country, preaching peace and demonstrating his teaching by action.

The weapon Shakyamuni used was none other than "nonviolent dialogue". Through dialogue he taught the sanctity of life and tried to eliminate violence from society.

Tehranian: Without dialogue, we will have to walk in the darkness of self-righteousness.

The Common Ground of Humanity

Ikeda: To borrow your metaphor, dialogue is a kind of light to illuminate one's footsteps. The whole thing begins with one human being talking with another. Inter-civilizational dialogue is currently the focus of attention, but the point of departure or the prototype is human-to-human rapport.

Whenever I visited socialist or communist countries during the Cold War years, I was always guided by the conviction that "because there are people to talk with" it must be possible to build a bridge of friendship.

We must somehow break through the "friend vs. foe" pattern of relationship and talk with each other honestly and openly on the common ground of humanity. That, I was firmly convinced, would break the ice and lead to problem solving in the end.

Tehranian: I'm well aware of your pioneering work in promoting dialogues. During the past 40 years, you have conducted over 1500 dialogues with world leaders, from Toynbee to Gorbachev.

Ikeda: Just as once there were strong prejudices against the socialist countries, today many people, especially those in Europe and North America, hold on to stereotypical images and biased preconceptions about the Islamic world. This is very dangerous.

Tehranian: I, too, am deeply concerned about the current situation. But you have taken the initiative in pursuing activities to prevent specific countries from being isolated in the international community.

Ikeda: To know each other well is the first step toward intimate friendship. To appreciate one's partner's strong points and to be ready to learn from him or her—this is required of all of us who live in the world today. I hope this series of dialogues between the two of us, one with a Buddhist background and the other from the Islamic tradition, will help encourage people to follow our example.

Rules for Dialogue

Tehranian: As I said earlier, the Toda Institute has chosen "Dialogue of Civilizations for World Citizenship" for its motto. As we groped for the most effective way to conduct dialogue, we have developed a set of rules. They are suggestive more than exhaustive, but I would like to introduce them here.

There are ten points:

- Honor others and listen to them deeply with your heart and mind.
- Seek common ground for consensus, but avoid "group-think" by acknowledging and honoring the diversity of views.
- Refrain from irrelevant or intemperate intervention.

- Acknowledge others' contributions to the discussion before making your own.
- Remember that silence also speaks; speak only when you have a contribution to make by posing a relevant question, presenting a fact, making or clarifying a point, or advancing the discussion to more specificity or greater consensus.
- Identify the critical points of difference for further discussion.
- Never distort other views in order to advance your own; try to restate the others' positions to their satisfaction before presenting your own differing views.
- Formulate agreements on each agenda item before moving on to the next.
- Draw out the implications of an agreement for group policy and action.
- Thank your colleagues for their contributions.

Ikeda: They are all important points. The common thread seems to be open dialogue based on respect for others. I think you have presented a highly valuable list of rules that will serve as a model for the kind of dialogue humankind should pursue from now on.

Men of Dialogue: Montaigne and Gandhi

Ikeda: It will be very useful to look back over history and see what some of the great figures had to say.

Along with Socrates, I would single out Montaigne as an outstanding "man of dialogue". As you know, he lived in 16th-century France in the midst of a succession of tragic incidents arising from religious conflict.

In *The Essays*, Montaigne says that the most effective and natural method of cultivating a strong mind is to carry on conversation. He calls talking together the most enjoyable of all human activities.

Tehranian: I, too, enjoy conversation for its own sake.

Ikeda: That's the hallmark of a pacifist. Montaigne goes on to say that no beliefs or convictions, even if they are miles apart from his own, can hurt him; no matter how turned or fantastic, he finds worth in anything that is a product of man's mental functions.

Tehranian: I can see some points quite similar to our rules.

Ikeda: Montaigne went by Cicero's famous aphorism, "There is no discussion with refutation", so he emphasized that the purpose of dialogue is none other than pursuit of truth. Four centuries later and far away from France, Mahatma Gandhi rejected all sorts of sectarianism, saying, "Truth is God". He consistently followed the principle of *ahimsa* (noninjury) in his actions in hopes of awakening all people of the world to the internal, spiritual power geared toward the sacred.

Tehranian: Speaking of Gandhi, I was very much impressed by your lecture at the Gandhi Memorial Hall in February, 1992. I, too believe that dialogue is closely related to what Gandhi called "*satyagraha*" (search for truth). I say this because *satyagraha* aims at directly appealing to people's innermost sense of morality.

Ikeda: Appealing to the innermost sense of morality—that means that the essence of dialogue lies in prompting the meeting of hearts and minds.

You cannot expect to persuade anyone if you try to impose your own ideas or beliefs on others in the name of dialogue. That kind of approach will only sow "the seeds of animosity", to borrow your phrase again. It will be impossible to bring people together, much less unite them.

We must continue to call for the need to expand dialogue at all levels, but at the same time we ought to keep working on ways to improve its methodology and quality. Only when these two kinds of efforts are simultaneously pursued will dialogue become a truly effective tool, powerful enough to make history.

CHAPTER 2

Islam

Understanding Islam as it Really is

Tehranian: I have traveled along the Silk Road. Though it was destroyed by European colonialism, the Silk Road once connected Asia and Europe, becoming the locus of the world's first "global economy" and "global culture".

Today, we are witnessing the formation of a "new global economy", but its intellectual and cultural counterparts—a global perspective and culture—have barely begun to emerge.

Mr. Ikeda, you have been actively involved in a pioneering effort to create a new global culture comparable to the global economy.

Ikeda: I agree wholeheartedly with your call urging the need to forge a new global culture, although I do not consider myself a pioneer in that effort.

You also mentioned the meeting of East and West, but what Islam is really like and how Muslims actually live are hardly known in the West, or in Japan for that matter. For instance, very few Japanese are even aware that banks operating in accordance with Islamic law are prohibited from paying interest on savings.

Tehranian: That is a customary practice based on the notion that amassing wealth without working is unfair and undesirable. The Koran explicitly forbids the practice of providing interest on savings (2.275).

Ikeda: I understand that many Muslims relinquish their right to interest payments on savings in non-Islamic banks, choosing instead to donate the payments to worthy causes or offer them as alms to the poor.

Tehranian: There are, of course, all sorts of rich Muslims, but I know quite a few who refuse to receive the interest they are entitled to. However, some Islamic bankers allow their depositors to become shareholders and receive dividends that are permitted by Islamic law.

13

Ikeda: Another widely held stereotyped image is that women are severely discriminated against in Islamic society. But actually the ratio of women among political leaders, government officials, and intellectuals is higher in Islamic countries than in Japan, for example. There is an Arab woman who studies at Soka University, always wearing a *hijab*. She is expected to pursue a professional career after she returns to her country.

"Make no judgment before you know the facts"—this was Tsune-saburo Makiguchi's basic stance of learning. Accurate perception of reality leads to fair evaluation. We must do away with our biases based on false or stereotyped images of Islam, and to that end we should first confirm some basic facts about it.

Tehranian: I vigorously support that position. Firsthand observation is increasingly more important in this day and age of electronic transmission of information, when people have little choice but to become passive recipients of ready-made information.

Ikeda: For about two weeks from the end of January, 1962, I visited Iran, your home country, and four other Islamic nations—Iraq, Turkey, Egypt, and Pakistan.

Japan, at that time, was in the midst of rapid economic growth; the whole economy was swinging upward with unprecedented speed. Very few Japanese ever questioned the supreme value of material "progress".

Going from our extremely secularized society to Islamic countries where religious traditions still weigh very heavily was shockingly refreshing to me. The whole atmosphere also made me feel nostalgic. It was during that trip that I was told Muslims divide time into three categories.

Tehranian: You mean *salat*, the time for prayer, *shoghl*, the time for labor, and *raha*, the time for play and pleasure.

Ikeda: Apparently, working hard to make money isn't valued so highly in Islamic society. By contrast, in the industrially advanced countries, leisure activities are largely for mental and physical refreshment to prepare one for the next workday, hence they are more a kind of *shoghl* than *raha* in the Islamic sense of the term.

Tehranian: For workaholics, everything is *shoghl*; even play and recreation are made subservient to work. Such people work for the sake of working, not for some larger goal in life.

Ikeda: The most highly valued category of time in Islam is *salat*, time spent in offering prayers to Allah, and *raha* discussing topics of interest with one's friends, traveling, composing poems, and, above all, pondering on the meaning of life. During my 1962 trip I sensed how such time for self-improvement flowed slowly but deeply among the people I saw.

Orientalism Reconsidered

Ikeda: The experience taught me how important it is to see another culture as it really is and to be honestly surprised, excited, or even electrified. People of our time tend to stand on guard whenever they come across something unfamiliar to them, labeling it "alien", "strange", or even "evil".

Tehranian: That's precisely what Edward Said called "Orientalism" and criticized the mentality as follows:

> "Men have always divided the world up into regions having either real or imagined distinction from each other. The absolute demarcation between East and West, which Balfour and Cromer accept with such complacency, had been years, or even centuries, in the making ... Many terms were used to express the relation [between East and West]. The Oriental is irrational, depraved (fallen), childlike, "different"; thus the European is rational, virtuous, mature, 'normal'."
> (Edward Said, *Orientalism*, 1979, pp. 39–40)

Ikeda: Evaluations of Said's interpretations vary among critics, but there is no doubt that his *Orientalism* was an epoch-making work. Both his opponents and supporters have had to take the book into consideration when they discuss Asia and colonialism.

He has been suffering from a serious disease—I believe it is leukemia—but he has consistently stood on the side of the minority. I have high regard for his strong willpower, articulateness, and action.

In any case, when someone discriminates against another person, the reason lies not with the victim but with the discriminator. It is not that the other person is inferior but that someone is psychologically conditioned to prejudice.

Tehranian: It is not really possible, in any case, to divide the world into such simple categories as "East" and "West". Many of the great religions—Judaism, Christianity, and Islam—originated in West Asia.

Ikeda: The religions that form the spiritual backbone of Western society were born in West Asia. Cultures are all mixed and blended.

Japan is indebted to other Asian countries for its Chinese-character-based orthography, Confucianism, Buddhism, and many other aspects of its culture.

Tehranian: There is no such thing as a "pure race" or a "pure nation", or even "pure religion". Such notions are nothing but dangerous illusions filled with prejudices.

Ikeda: The 20th century has witnessed many tragedies repeated over and over because people are often driven by such illusions.

For many years I have been conducting dialogues with people of different cultural, ethnic, and religious backgrounds, including this one with yourself. My motivation is simply to encounter and mutually stimulate a dialogue that expands the multidimensional network of exchange for peace on a global scale.

Judaism, Christianity, and Islam

Ikeda: Islam's position on the relationship among Judaism, Christianity, and Islam is clearly stated in the Koran. For one thing, it claims that the three are but manifestations of the same religion in different historical contexts.[1]

Tehranian: That is right. Judaism, Christianity, and Islam are sometimes called "Abrahamic" religions because of the reverence all three religions hold for the founder of monotheism in their tradition. Zoroastrians also have a legitimate claim to monotheism. That is why after the Islamic conquest of Persia, Zoroastrianism also was recognized by Muslims as a Religion of the Book.

Ikeda: For another thing, Islam claims that its founder Muhammad is a prophet like Moses and Jesus, and that he is the last of the numerous prophets sent by God, i.e. "the culmination and fulfillment of prophecies".

Tehranian: That is correct.

The Life of Muhammad: The Revelations He Received

Ikeda: Let us take a brief look at the life of Prophet Muhammad. It is said that he was born around 570 A.D. into the ruling tribe of Qureish in Mecca. He lost his father before birth, and his mother passed away when he was only six years old. So he was raised by his uncle.

Tehranian: Right. As an orphan, Muhammad experienced many trials—the pain and suffering of the destitute, the early death of his parents—which certainly had a great impact on his childhood.

Then, when he was twenty-five, Muhammad married an older, rich widow, Khadija, who entrusted him with her fortune.

Ikeda: Muhammad, nevertheless, continued to be very conscious of the poverty he had experienced. It remained as a kind of thorn in his heart that he could not simply put aside. We find many passages in the Koran admonishing people to take care of orphans, the poor, and the alone.

Tehranian: Yes. In a chapter entitled "The Morning Hours", we find the following:

> "Did He [Thy Lord] not find thee an orphan and protect (thee)?
> Did He not find thee wandering and direct (thee)?
> Did He not find thee destitute and enrich (thee)?" (93. 6–8)

Ikeda: Another Koranic passage that well expresses Muhammad's sensitivity goes:

> "Know that the life of this world is only play, and idle talk, and pageantry, and boasting among you, and rivalry in respect of wealth and children." (57.20)

Actually, Shakyamuni, the founder of Buddhism, too, felt an existential "thorn" in his heart in his youth. Though born as a prince, Shakyamuni lost his mother only a week after his birth. Economically, he was able to lead a luxurious life, but he always felt unsettled about the wide gap between rich and poor, the extravagance of court life, and other contradictions in society.

When I look at the life of great religious founders, I find that they had two kinds of extraordinary sensitivities—one for the suffering of others, and the other for that which is eternal.

Tehranian: In Buddhist terminology, they are "compassion" and "wisdom", aren't they?

Ikeda: You are right, indeed.

Now back to Muhammad. He soon began to immerse himself often in meditation. Like many of his contemporaries, he periodically retreated into a mountain cave. One night in 610 A.D., he is said to have heard the Angel Jibrail (Gabriel in the Old Testament) commanding him, "Read in the name of your great God".

Tehranian: For more than twenty years after that until his death, Muhammad continued to receive revelations intermittently. The sum total of these revelations is what is known as the Koran.

Some people may laugh at the idea of "divine" revelation as being unscientific. In fact, disparaging a religious experience as "unscientific" is indeed "unscientific". The language of revelations is symbolic akin to the language of poetry.

Ikeda: To use modern social science terminology, "revelation" is a kind of "ideal type". It might also be termed a "system of expression."

Take Pablo Picasso, for example. The uniquely deformed shapes in his paintings are an expression of his artistic inspiration. One cannot argue that his human faces are not biologically accurate without being laughed at for lack of artistic sense.

Tehranian: I should think so. In fact, Picasso looked at reality from several different perspectives. Cubism thus provides a multi-dimensional view of reality.

Ikeda: The Old Testament says that God created human beings in his own image, an idea that is diametrically opposed to the theory of evolution. Yet, faith in the Creation has led to belief in the sanctity of human life, which in turn has motivated many individuals to devote themselves to the peace movement or become conscientious objectors.

On the other hand, others have distorted evolutionary theory in order to rationalize racism, ethnocentrism and even ethnic cleansing. Obviously, these latter people are more irrational and unscientific than the faithful.

Tehranian: The important point to acknowledge is that all of the great religious leaders in history have proved themselves to be extraordinary people with inspired messages that have guided humanity toward happier lives.

The Birth of Islam

Ikeda: When Muhammad received the first revelation, he was shocked and bewildered in disbelief. In fact, his wife, Khadija, had to encourage him to believe in the truth of the revelation and devote himself to serving as God's messenger. She was the first person to join the newfound faith.

Tehranian: People of Mecca, however, did not first accept the teaching Muhammad was trying to spread.

Ikeda: As I understand it, Mecca was flourishing in those days as a major junction in trade routes connecting China and India, on the one hand, and areas along the Mediterranean coast, on the other. That meant that there was a wide gap between the rich and the poor in the city.

According to the well-known Japanese Orientalist Dr. Toshihiko Izutsu, the life ethics of people in those days was based on the notion that "everything is determined by the past" (Izutsu, T., *Isuramu seitan* [The Birth of Islam], Chuo Koronsha Bunko, 1990, p. 27). "The past" here refers to "the path of life that their forebears had trod for hundreds of years", (Ibid.), that is, *sunna* in Arabic.

Tehranian: The mores of the kinship community were the dominant social norms. Muhammad's reformist ideas were regarded as a threat to the Meccan aristocracy.

Ikeda: Wealthy, conservative people naturally considered Muhammad potentially subversive of the established social order, but the poor and ordinary people supported him. It is said that he had a large following among young people.

The ruling authorities that had at first ignored or even ridiculed Muhammad soon found him a force to be reckoned with and began to persecute him and his followers.

Tehranian: That's right. They realized the revolutionary nature of Muhammad's message. Many of his followers and their families sought refuge in Ethiopia and other places.

To make matters worse, Khadija, who had been his strongest supporter, died. His uncle, Abu Talib, who had raised Muhammad, also passed away soon afterward.

Ikeda: In both his religious and private life, Muhammad was beset with the greatest difficulties.

Tehranian: Exactly. Following his persecution in Mecca, Muhammad took a bold step by fleeing to Medina, where he had virtually no following. This flight to Medina is known as *Hegira*. The Islamic calendar begins with *Hegira*, rather than with Muhammad's birth. It signifies the start of the Islamic Era.

Ikeda: Muhammad achieved almost miraculous success in Medina, where he spent a little more than eleven years until his death.

How would you explain Muhammad's tremendous success in a place where he had virtually no personal contacts?

Tehranian: Prior to Muhammad's exodus to Medina, there had been incessant fighting in many parts of the peninsula among the warring Arab tribes. Medina was no exception; there, several powerful Jewish and Arab tribes had been in rivalry for years. Muhammad was chosen as mediator.

Ikeda: Why did people in Medina choose him for the role?

Tehranian: Well, Muhammad had a wide reputation as an honest man. He was called Amin, i.e. trustworthy. That is why they invited him to mediate among them.

Ikeda: When he was still a merchant in obscurity, Muhammad was respected as a man of sincerity by people in Mecca. It was his personal integrity, then, that rescued him from extreme adversity and provided him with a new setting for activity in Medina. The whole episode shows that his noble character was the great asset that supported him in crisis.

Islamic Civilization: Faith, Diversity, and Pursuit of Knowledge

Ikeda: Let me ask you another question at this point. What is *the* characteristic of Islamic civilization?

Tehranian: In one word, the essence of Islamic civilization is faith and unity in diversity.

Ikeda: In the United States today, Muslims are engaged in a variety of unique creative activities. In Europe, too, Islamic culture is exerting vigorous influence in music and many other fields. I, for one, have great interest in the whole of Islamic civilization.

Tehranian: Islamic civilization was built upon four pillars: religion, law, science, and culture. Of these, the religious dimension was powerfully represented in the Koranic verse: "Let there be no compulsion in religion" (2.257).

This and other verses inspired a belief in the unity of creation without imposing any particular religion on people. This religious view also gave rise to an Islamic legal system that allowed considerable diversity.

Ikeda: The word *Sharia* (Divine Law) originally meant "the way to a watering place", which connotes "the way to salvation". Thus, the Islamic Law could be seen more as the way of conduct people should observe as human beings than as the legal system of a nation-state.

Tehranian: Science soon became a third pillar of Islam on the basis of Prophet Muhammad's pronouncement that every Muslim man and woman must seek knowledge "even unto China".

Ikeda: Cultural interchange between China and the Islamic world began long before the age of the Great Voyages in Europe.

Tehranian: At that time, China was perhaps the remotest part of Arab geographic imagination. Muslim scholars and scientists thus appropriated Persian, Egyptian, Greek, Indian, and Chinese scientific contributions without hesitation or apology as part of God's wonderful mysteries to be discovered and employed.

Ikeda: Islam in China reminds me of "Aladdin and the Wonderful Lamp". It is a legend, of course, but Aladdin, a poor Chinese boy, finds a wonderful lamp whose magical power enables him to become China's ruler. The fairy tale version is much simplified, but the original story tells us something about the growth of Islam in China.

Tehranian: Very true. The Islamic world became the leading scientific and technological center of the world from the ninth to the thirteenth centuries.

Ikeda: It is well known that the Islamic world highly valued Greek and Roman philosophy and other branches of learning.

Tehranian: Islam enriched itself and the rest of the world, not by destroying other cultures but by incorporating them.

Ikeda: That is one of the important lessons we have to learn from the history of Islamic civilization. Absorbing other cultures is indeed the best way to enrich your own.

Relations with Medieval Europe

Tehranian: In other genres of cultural production, the Islamic world was highly advanced, including things that directly contribute to the enrichment of daily life.

Ikeda: Many scientific terms originate in either Arabic or Persian, such as alcohol, alkali, ammonia, and aniline. And words for daily necessities, foods and plants stem from the same sources—pajamas, jungle, paradise, cotton, sofa, magazine, lemon, orange, syrup, tulip, to give just a few examples.

Tehranian: Some metaphysical concepts such as "paradise" and "satan" also originate from Persian and Arabic. From the 8th to the 9th centuries, most of the extant Greek texts, including those of Aristotle, were translated into Arabic.

Ikeda: Translation was obviously undertaken as a religious project. The fruits of the Hellenistic civilization and other works of ancient Mediterranean science, philosophy, and knowledge were not transmitted directly to Europe. The massive influx of Germanic tribes was followed in Europe by a long period of feudalism. The heritage of Greek/Roman civilization was preserved and developed in the meantime by the Islamic world.

Tehranian: It was not until the 11th century, when Europeans began active exchange with the "Orient", that the fruits of advanced Islamic civilization were introduced into Europe.

Ikeda: The imported Islamic science and culture thus played a crucial role in the Renaissance that took place in Europe a few centuries later. The Renaissance meant revival of ancient or classical art and literature that had been long forgotten in Europe. In that sense, Islam was a great benefactor of the European Renaissance.

Tehranian: Along with the works of Aristotle and other Greek scholars, those of Ibn Rushd, Ibn Sina, and other Islamic philosophers were transmitted to Europe. They were instrumental in the development of medieval Christian theology.

Ikeda: Right. Ibn Rushd's name was Latinized as Averroes, and Ibn Sina as Avicenna. Their works were widely read by European philosophers and theologians.

The works of Ibn Rushd, in particular, gave rise to a school of theologians called Latin Averroists, who exerted a great influence on the Christian community in Europe.

Tehranian: Europe in the Middle Ages was fragmented into a series of self-contained feudal principalities. By contrast, the Islamic empires during the same period enjoyed considerable mobility of trade and people across vast regions that brought scholars into contact with the sources of learning. In this context, the role of Jewish and Christian scholars should not be overlooked.

Ikeda: In Baghdad, the capital of the Abbassids, there was a Jewish academy named Yeshiva, where research on and compilation of the Talmud were undertaken. Records show that active exchange of views took place between the Jewish rabbis there and the *ulema*, scholars of the Islamic law.

Tehranian: Because Islam showed tolerance, scholars and scientists of whatever background could enter into dialogue and exchange. The examples of Islamic and Christian Spain are telling.

Ikeda: After Islam conquered Spain in the 8th century, places like Cordoba and Granada became academic centers where Europeans could study advanced Islamic culture, science and the arts. Especially Granada, known for the beautiful Alhambra palace, drew many Jewish students.

Tehranian: But as soon as the Muslims were expelled from Spain in 1492, so were the Jews, and the Inquisition against Christian heretics followed. The lesson of this episode is clear:

Diversity is a source of cultural vitality; uniformity leads to cultural stagnation.

Ikeda: On the negation of diversity, Theodor W. Adorno writes, "Auschwitz has demonstrated the validity of the philosophical proposition that pure uniformity equals death" (*Negative Dialektik*, 1967, trans. G. Kida, 1996).

Life is another name for diversity. Standardization or uniformity means death. In this day and age of increasing cultural uniformity, it is all the more important, I believe, for us to respect diverse cultures and grope for their coexistence.

Tehranian: I agree. I hope this dialogue provides support for such efforts.

Note

1. The following passages in the Koran exemplify this point.

   "Dispute ye with us concerning Allah when He is our Lord and your Lord? ... We look to Him alone. (2.139)

   We believe in Allah and that which is revealed unto us and that which was revealed unto Abraham, and Ishmael, and Isaac, and Jacob, and the tribes, and that which Moses and Jesus received, and that which the Prophets received from their Lord. We make no distinction between any of them, and unto Him we have surrendered. (2.136)

   Those who (formerly) received the Scripture differed only after knowledge came unto them, through transgression among themselves." (3.19)

CHAPTER 3

Buddhism

Tehranian: As I see it, Nichiren Buddhism and Islam share some common characteristics. Both attach importance to history, for example. By contrast, some Hindu and Christian sects do not consider history particularly relevant to their teachings. Another common feature of Islam and Nichiren Buddhism is their emphasis on this world, on secular reality. As you know, some religions are oriented more heavily toward Heaven or the afterworld than life in this world.

Shakyamuni's Motive for Taking the Tonsure

Tehranian: This time I would like to learn more about Buddhism from you, Mr. Ikeda. And I hope that in the course of our discussion, the similarities and differences between Islam and Buddhism will become evident. Of course, we will not interpret in negative terms whatever differences we may find between the two.

Ikeda: "Difference" can mean "diversity". Similarities provide a basis for cooperation, but we must also be aware of our differences, ready to respect each religion's role and the strengths of the other. Then we will find ways we can each contribute to the world.

The "parable of the three kinds of medicinal herbs and two kinds of trees", cited in the fifth chapter of the Lotus Sutra, demonstrates how impartially the Buddha expounds truth for all people but how differently they understand and benefit from it, depending on their respective abilities. Life-giving rain, the parable goes, falls equally on all plants, trees, herbs, etc., but they absorb the moisture differently and grow to varying heights according to their individual nature. Likewise, the Buddha's teachings help people grow in a variety of ways, thereby guaranteeing the diversity of lives and cultures. Diversity is the proof of life.

Tehranian: As we agreed in our previous discussion, uniformity is a symbol of death.

Now, let me begin by asking you some questions about Gautama Buddha's life and the historical significance of his thought.

Ikeda: Gautama Buddha is popularly known as Shakyamuni (Shakuson in Japanese). "Shakya" derives from the name of the tribe he was born into and "muni" stands for sage or saint. So let me call him Shakyamuni instead of Gautama Buddha.

The great Indian poet Tagore has the following to say about Shakyamuni:

> In India, Shakyamuni made man a great being. He did not approve of the caste system, liberated people from the ritual of sacrificial offering, and removed God from the purview of human goals. Shakyamuni revealed man's innate strength and tried to bring about blessings and happiness from within man rather than seeking them in Heaven. With deep respect and affection for humanity, Shakyamuni praised wisdom, power, zeal and other qualities inherent in man. In this way, he proclaimed that man is *not* a trifle, a miserable being buffeted by destiny. (Translated from *Tagoru chosaku-shu* [Selected Works of Tagore], vol. 7, Daisan Bunmei-sha, 1986, pp. 467–68)

Tehranian: The passage brilliantly shows the great poet's intuitive grasp of the essence of Buddhism. In effect, the Buddha freed humankind from the spell of magical religion and put happiness in the hands of people not threatened by the quirks of fate.

Ikeda: Exactly. Human beings are not creatures made sport of by fate, not trivial existences tossed about on rough waves. Each person possesses an infinite potential that makes anything possible. This was indeed Shakyamuni's declaration of human independence.

Tehranian: In the previous chapter, you mentioned that even though he was born as a prince, young Shakyamuni abandoned the secular world to take the tonsure. In Sufism, there is a legend about Ibrahim Adham, a king who renounced his crown and worldly possessions to seek spiritual enlightenment. The story parallels Shakyamuni's life. I would like you to explain to me what motivated him to make that decision. With all his wealth and youthful vigor, why did he renounce everything?

Ikeda: The following passages in a sutra called *Anguttara-Nikáya* give a fairly accurate account of what motivated Shakyamuni to take the tonsure in his youth:

> I was thus quite well to do and quite tenderhearted and vulnerable, but then the following thoughts occurred to me:

A foolish ordinary mortal, even though he too is bound to grow old and cannot escape from aging, becomes contemplative, annoyed, ashamed, and disgusted when he sees others growing senile, excluding himself.

A foolish ordinary mortal, even though he too is bound to get sick and cannot escape from illness, becomes contemplative, annoyed, ashamed, and disgusted when he sees others who are sick, excluding himself.

A foolish ordinary mortal, even though he too is bound to die and cannot escape from death, becomes contemplative, annoyed, ashamed, and disgusted when he sees others dying, excluding himself.

Thinking along these lines, Shakyamuni felt the "arrogance of being youthful, healthy, and alive" disappear from his mind.

Tehranian: So, the Buddha's motive for taking the tonsure was that he squarely faced the four sufferings of birth, old age, sickness, and death that inevitably affect all human beings, wasn't it?

To be sure, suffering visits not just people of tragedy and misfortune; it is an integral part of human existence.

Ikeda: It is noteworthy that Shakyamuni uses the word "arrogance" for suffering. It is the arrogance of looking askance at others in terms of their age or ill health that is the source of all sorts of human suffering.

The important thing to remember here is that Shakyamuni did *not* abandon the secular world in order to escape from such suffering. His awareness of suffering led him rather to search for the causes. In other words, Shakyamuni's renunciation of secular life was not an "escape" from suffering but an attempt to identify its causes and find ways to overcome it.

That is why Shakyamuni is described as a winner in the Buddhist sutras. He was *not* a hermit but a fighter, a perennial victor.

Tehranian: So his motivation was not pessimism, was it?

Ikeda: Just before his death, Shakyamuni told his disciples that he left the secular world at the age of twenty-nine "in search of goodness" (*Dîgha-Nikâya*).

I think that the expression "in search of" merits our attention. It suggests no hint of pessimism whatsoever.

Shakyamuni realized the truth that the egoism lurking in the deepest layers of the human psyche—the arrogance of distinguishing between young and old, healthy and sickly, and living and dead—was the ultimate source of suffering. His renunciation of the secular life was in fact a declaration of war against human suffering.

Buddhism and Sufism

Tehranian: I have been interested in various world religions and have studied them in my own way. As I mentioned at the outset of our discussion, I find a lot of similarities between Buddhism and Sufism, which is Islamic mysticism.

Your own interpretation of Mahayana Buddhism closely corresponds to the Sufi worldview. Both religions focus on the fragility and transience of life and worldly pursuits. Both emphasize human responsibility and inner life. Both worldviews avoid religious dogma and are open to ecumenical dialogue with all faiths, ideologies, and philosophies.

Ikeda: I know what you mean. Professor Nur Yalman of Harvard University said to me during a discussion, "I believe that Sufism was substantively affected by its encounter with Buddhism, incorporating the latter's idea of meditation and other elements into its system of thought."

Tehranian: That would make sense. Neither religion negates the meaning of secular life. Both encourage their followers to take time for spiritual retreats and contemplation, but that does not mean withdrawal from the cares of this world. Rather, they both call for a strong moral commitment to social service, and they both believe in the human obligation to "pursue good", as you have put it.

One notable difference, I would say, is the absence of a priesthood in Sufism, but in both traditions, the individual directly faces the ultimate source of all existence.

Ikeda: Nichiren Buddhism is known for its idea of "establishing the peace of the land for the correct teaching". As a Buddhist you must always be involved in society and ready to lead people through the nobility of your character. Shakyamuni, too, exhorted his disciples to "throw yourselves in the midst of people for the sake of their happiness and benefits". A Buddha does not just sit idly in meditation but walks among the masses, telling them about the way of happiness.

Tehranian: What you say reminds me of a Sufi poem written by Sa'adi, a great 13th-century Persian poet:

"To pray is nothing but serving humanity.
Prayer rugs, rosaries, and begging bowls are but vanity."

I am completely in agreement with you that Buddhism is a "religion of hope" free from all bondage. That is also true of Sufism. That is why they are so suited to meeting the conditions of the contemporary world, in which no dogma can match the enormous diversity of humankind or keep pace with emerging challenges.

Ikeda: I can see your point very well. Dogma represents the state of being bound up in the narrow, petty fetters of the ego. By working for the benefit of humanity and by serving people, we can free ourselves from such fetters.

Characteristics of Nichiren Buddhism

Ikeda: So far we have talked about Shakyamuni's life and the essence of Buddhism. At this point, let me say a few things about the Nichiren Buddhism that I believe in.

Tehranian: I am very eager to hear what you have to say on the subject, because I want to understand the philosophical base of the Soka Gakkai movement for peace and human rights and the vigorous enthusiasm with which members carry on their activities.

Ikeda: Nichiren's lifetime (1222–82) coincided with a major turning point in Japanese history. Politically, the aristocratic ruling structure centered on the emperor and court nobility was being replaced by a military regime controlled by the warrior class, but not without large-scale civil wars and social unrest that only increased the miseries of the general populace. Devastating earthquakes, famine, and epidemics frequently occurred, deepening and aggravating the situation.

Meanwhile, the Mongol Empire was rapidly expanding its sphere of influence in East Asia. Threatened from outside and desolated within, Japanese society was permeated by tension and a mood of eschatology.

Tehranian: Great ideas usually appear in such times of political and moral crisis.

Ikeda: At the age of thirty-nine (1260), Nichiren wrote a lengthy letter of remonstration, submitted to the most powerful leader of the ruling Hojo clan. Entitled "On Establishing the Correct Teaching for the Peace of the Land", the treatise articulated his view that religion should contribute to the construction of a peaceful land more than the repose of the individual's soul in the afterlife.

Tehranian: Clearly, Nichiren was heir to the characteristics of Mahayana Buddhism that you explained earlier. In his approach, I find an ideal relationship between society and religion, between political and religious institutions. That is, while adhering to the principle of separation, the two institutions can still monitor and stimulate one another. They can check and balance each other through the creative tension between ideals and reality. Politics can be chastened by religious ideals, while religion itself is kept apart from the inevitable rough-and-tumble of political life.

Ikeda: "Creative tension"—that is an apt phrase. Josei Toda, too, admonished us to "Keep close watch over politics!"

It is not only our right but our duty as well to carefully monitor politics and try to guide it in the right direction from the standpoint of the religious ideals of peace, the protection of the weak, etc. We must perform this legitimate duty both as persons of religion and as citizens.

Tehranian: The Soka Gakkai movement in Japan seems to me to have achieved this creative balance between religious and political life and institutions. By separating the religious organization from the political parties it supports, it has reserved its own right to review and criticize their failures in matters of public policy.

Ikeda: That is very true. The members of the Soka Gakkai are very strict with their politicians. That was one of my mentor's teachings, and we faithfully observe it.

Tehranian: Insofar as the Soka Gakkai maintains the right to be critical of politics and its institutions, by supporting certain policies and parties, the religious organization can influence society to move toward the religious ideals of Soka Gakkai—peace and social justice. In this respect, engaged Buddhism, as exemplified by Soka Gakkai, and engaged Islam have much in common.

Ikeda: To go back to Nichiren, an outspoken prophet like him could not have been favored by those in positions of power. He had to undergo persecution and official oppression. He was sent into exile twice during his lifetime. Through these experiences, however, Nichiren became convinced that he was a "votary of the Lotus Sutra".

During his exile on the forbiddingly cold, northern island of Sado, Nichiren wrote many of his important works, including "Kaimoku Sho" [The Opening of the Eyes]. In it, Nichiren reviews history in terms of those who protected the people (the sovereign), those who led the people spiritually (teachers), and those who love people as parents love their children (parents).

Nichiren's conclusion is that Shakyamuni himself was the most outstanding in the three virtues of sovereign, teacher, and parent. Nichiren goes on to declare himself to be the heir to Shakyamuni's spirit because he is propagating the Law that Buddhahood is inherent in all sentient beings, despite all sorts of persecution and oppression.

Tehranian: In Nichiren's presentation, I see evidence of objective reasoning, an intellectual effort not to fall into an arbitrary argument. Above all, his focus of attention is clearly set on people.

Ikeda: Nichiren always employed three kinds of evidence in presenting his arguments: Documentary evidence (what the sutras say); theoretical evidence (compatibility with reason and logic); and actual evidence (the content of a doctrine or assertion being borne out in the context of reality). In other words, Nichiren was in constant dialogue with the Buddha, with reason, and with reality, making certain that he was not trapped in dogma. It was through such meticulous verification of his arguments that Nichiren arrived at an in-depth understanding of the spirit of the Lotus Sutra, i.e., the equality of all sentient beings, and tried to put it into practice among the people.

Tehranian: I am most grateful for your account of Nichiren's turbulent life and profound teachings. His intensity of purpose, purity of intentions, passionate pursuit of justice and equality, emphasis on a believer's direct access to the sources of divine inspiration without the intervention of clergy—all spell out a religious tradition that is surprisingly modern and democratic. In Sufism, too, purity of intention (*safaye batin*) is the supreme test of our actions.

In many respects, Nichiren's life resembles that of Prophet Muhammad. The opposition to Nichiren's teachings by the authorities of the time also resembles the stiff opposition that Muhammad faced in Mecca from the ruling tribes. Like Nichiren, Muhammad has continued to be subjected to vilification as a fanatic. But that is not surprising. Their messages will continue to be threatening to the ruling classes who prefer people to be submissive and incapable of spiritual and political self-confidence.

Ikeda: In a letter written in 1277 to a follower, Nichiren writes, "When a tiger roars, gales blow; when a dragon intones, clouds gather. Yet a hare's squeal or a donkey's bray causes neither wind nor clouds to arise" (*Letters of Nichiren*, Columbia University Press, 1996 p. 460).

Nichiren saw everything in broad perspective, dealing with any situation with total presence of mind.

The Contemporary Role of Buddhism and Islam

Ikeda: Let us now consider what perspectives the two religions—Buddhism and Islam—can offer the social problems of our time.

One of the major problems besetting contemporary society is the loss of respect for the eternal and universal. Individualism has made advances while universalism has retreated. Without the backing of a wholesome outlook on the universal, individualism can easily degenerate into indifference toward others and cold-heartedness. I am seriously worried about the spread of cynicism in today's world.

"Whichever way things go, it makes no difference", people say. This kind of popular apathy may, in the end, allow something terribly evil to run rampant.

Tehranian: You have rightly identified our own time as an "age of confusion" and an "age of cynicism". Some have labeled it as the Postmodern Age; others have called it the Hypermodern Age. Whatever we call it, certain features of our own period of history stand out.

First, this is an age of acceleration of history. Events that used to take centuries or decades to unfold, nowadays take place within a few years or weeks, often right before our eyes on television.

Ikeda: Speed itself is a symbol of our time. Information comes and goes on the TV screen with astonishing speed, giving us not actual but vicarious experiences. People often feel closer to TV personalities than to their real neighbors. We may be living in an age when we do not have any direct experience, when everything is vicarious.

Tehranian: The positive aspect of acceleration of history is, for example, that it took two world wars to destroy the old European colonial empires. It took only a decade to undo the Soviet empire through peaceful dialogue. Similarly, the dictatorships in Iran, the Philippines, and Eastern Europe were unseated within a few years. Global communication has made it difficult for any dictatorial regime to last very long.

The negative aspect is that acceleration of history gives rise to what Alvin Toffler has called "future shock", and a desperate search for the "security blankets" and fetishisms of identity and commodity.

Ikeda: In a society overflowing with information, people are too absorbed in selecting new information that leaves human beings spiritually atrophied.

Tehranian: The spread of hypermodernism is atomizing societies. Selfish pursuits are taking the place of religious faith or civic mindedness. That, in turn, is leading to radical skepticism and cynicism. Existential mistrust, in which the motivations of everyone are questioned, is taking the place of bonds of social trust and solidarity.

Ikeda: Exactly. Voices of moderation and common sense are unheeded, while dangerous ultra-nationalism and religious fanaticism are gaining momentum.

Tehranian: Hypermodern societies have become vulnerable to what De Tocqueville (1805–59) aptly called "the tyranny of the majority". Authoritarian democracies are gradually taking the place of liberal democracies in the West and traditional dictatorships in the East. Under the guise of neo-conservatism, the new regimes combine economic liberalism with social conservatism and political authoritarianism to gain popular legitimacy without sacrificing special interests. Some have called this phenomenon "fascism with a smiling face".

Ikeda: This kind of new political power gives people a measure of material, mundane satisfaction as well as indifference to others in distress. Such an approach only accelerates a contemptuous attitude toward religious beliefs that value consideration for the well being of others.

Tehranian: Is there any hope in this new Dark Age? I believe there is. The hope lies in those religious (SGI being a prime example) and secular movements that are maintaining an ecumenical attitude toward "the others"—movements that are inclusive rather than exclusive.

Globalization requires a new type of Universalism, a theory and practice that begins with the acknowledgment of similarities before it starts to negotiate through dialogue the differences. In contrast to the European Enlightenment, which started with some abstract universal principles, the new Universalism must acknowledge, respect, and celebrate human diversity.

Death is homogeneity; life is heterogeneity. My motto for the new age is, therefore, the famous French motto, "*Vive la différence!*"

Ikeda: We have had more than enough experience during this century to realize that the old type of universalism was actually a kind of uniformity.

In the latter half of the Lotus Sutra, we find all sorts of bodhisattvas appear on the scene—people of intelligence, devotees, good singers, those whose kernel of faith is respect for others, and so on. The sutra foretells the advent of an age in which diversity flourishes and exhorts us to devote ourselves to the task of bringing about such an age.

The message of the Lotus Sutra is that humans, races, and nations all acknowledge their respective uniqueness and thrive together in peace by giving full play to individuality.

Tehranian: It seems to me that the Lotus Sutra is "an ode to diversity" in the real sense of the term. Rúmi's *Masnavi* is similarly a poetic tribute to diversity in religious beliefs and ethnic differences. He says:

> It often happens that a Turk and a Hindu speak the same language
> It also often happens that two Turks are strangers to each other
> The language of the heart is thus something unique
> The language of empathy is superior to language of the tongue.

CHAPTER 4

Buddhist-Islamic Encounters

Ikeda: So far, we've talked about the history of Islam, characteristics of Islamic thought, and comparisons with Buddhism. When this dialogue was serialized in the Ushio Magazine in 1998–2000, the reader response to our discussion was very positive. Quite a few people expressed the desire to know more about the basic tenets of Islam and what Muslims practice daily. So, I would like you to explain more about the Islamic doctrine.

First of all, what is the object of your faith? Christians, for example, believe in Jesus, the Savior, and the Holy Trinity. Sometimes people worship Virgin Mary too.

Tehranian: In a chapter in the Koran, we find the following passage: "O ye who believe! Believe in Allah and His messenger and the Scripture which He hath revealed unto His messenger and the Scripture which He revealed aforetime" (IV. 136). The creed of Islam is summarized in this passage.

Ikeda: In other words, the objects of Islamic faith are Allah, the Prophet Muhammad, the Koran, which records the revelation he received, the Torah of Judaism, and the Christian New Testament.

Many of our readers will probably be surprised to learn that Muslims treasure the Jewish and Christian scriptures as well.

Tehranian: According to the Islamic way of thinking, Judaism, Christianity, and Islam are called "Abrahamic religions" because their monotheistic faith goes back to the same founder.

These three religions enunciate belief in the same God. The Torah, the book of Mosaic Law, is the message God sent to humankind through Moses [*Musa* in Arabic], and the Christian New Testament, the book of Gospels, is the word of God conveyed through Jesus [*Issa* in Arabic]. The book of Psalms, too, was God's gift given via David.

Ikeda: The Law, Psalms, and Gospels—they correspond basically to the Old and New Testaments, don't they?

Tehranian: The Koran through Muhammad continues God's revelation to His prophets. God has sent many prophets to guide humanity from Adam to Muhammad. Jews and Christians are called "People of the Book" [*Ahl-al-kitab*] in Islam.

Ikeda: Muhammad criticized Judaism and Christianity not because their followers were worshipping a false god but because their faith in God had weakened.

Tehranian: That's right. The Jewish and Christian scriptures are essentially the same as the Koran. Therefore, both Jews and Christians will be saved in Heaven as long as they believe in God and the Last Judgment. But according to some Islamic views, their interpretation of the scriptures is erroneous and arbitrary. God revealed the Koran in order to rectify their mistaken beliefs.

Ikeda: In that sense, the birth of Islam was not so much the advent of a new religion as a kind of reformation calling on the "People of the Book" to "return to the Abrahamic religion" and reappraisal of their faith in God. It was a 7th-century reformation way ahead of Martin Luther's.

Tehranian: I see what you mean. Prophet Muhammad criticized Christianity of his time as follows:

> They have taken as lords beside Allah their rabbis and their monks and the Messiah son of Mary, when they were bidden to worship only One God. (IX.31)

Ikeda: Henry Corbin (1903–78), in his *History of Islamic Philosophy*, says something to the effect that in Islam there is no single clergyman whose job it is to intermediate grace, no Father, no Papal authority, not even a Council that makes decisions on doctrinal issues.

I'd like to confirm this point, but is it true that there is no clergy in Islam standing between God and the people?

Tehranian: That is correct. There is no hierarchy in Islam. We have no such things as a head temple or cathedral. Nor do we have anything like the Council of the Catholic Church that decides on questions of official doctrine.

Ikeda: There are mosques all over the world. Who are in charge of their management and how are they administered?

36

Tehranian: The Catholic churches throughout the world are under the control of the Vatican, whereas the mosques are run by the local community where they are located.

Ikeda: I have one more question. In Islam there are people called "ulama". They must be religious leaders; you see them on TV every now and then. Are they not priests or clergymen?

Tehranian: It is true that the *ulama* are engaged in research on and interpretation of the Koran, and they also teach the believers. They do things that priests or clergymen do in other religions, but they do *not* act as intermediaries between God and people. There are no ranks among them, either, although the weight of their pronouncements and the respect they command differ depending on their level of scholarship. In some branches of Islam such as Shi'ism, a definite clerical hierarchy has developed.

The *ulama* are representatives of various social strata and communities. They are leaders among people in a community, and their role in society is to voice the views and opinions of the people they represent.

Ikeda: I see. Prophet Muhammad did point out the decadence of the Jewish rabbis and Christian priests he actually saw.

Tehranian: Yes, he did, indeed. The Koranic chapter on repentance says:

> Lo! Many of the (Jewish) rabbis and the (Christian) monks devour the wealth of mankind wantonly and debar (men) from the way of Allah. (IX.34)

Ikeda: The prophet's vehement criticism of the corrupt clergy reminds me of Luther's reformation. In pursuit of *sola fides* (faith only!), he sought direct union with God without the mediation of the Church or the clergy and the return to the Bible. It was in that sense that I described the emergence of Islam as the 7th-century reformation.

Tehranian: There's much truth in what you've just said. I agree with your observation. Islam reasserted the equality of believers in the sight of God.

Ikeda: "Return to the beginning!"—As long as we keep in mind Prophet Muhammad's call, we will never fall into the trap of fanaticism.

Jesus, Muhammad, and Shakyamuni all sought the liberation of people. They inspired those in distress and helped the sick. Nichiren did the same. If we all returned to the great founders' humanitarian point of departure, we would be able to overcome conflict and strife.

Our Soka Gakkai movement, too, began with a call for "return to the Daishonin's time!" But the priesthood, so preoccupied with their prestige and authority, has done everything possible to obstruct our movement.

Josei Toda, my mentor and the second president of Soka Gakkai, used to say to us: "All problems will be solved if only the founders of the world's religions and schools of philosophy would get together to talk things out."

Tehranian: Fanaticism often arises when people's confidence in their faith is shaken due to rapid modernization or other similar phenomena. Hafez has said it all. "Excuse the war of seventy-two nations, failing to see the truth, they took the road to fantasies."

Ikeda: Because of Islam's regional orientation, Muslims of the world have different characteristics. American cultural anthropologist Clifford Geertz has shown how vastly different the Muslims of Morocco are from those of Indonesia. What is the common thread that makes all these diverse Muslims still Muslims?

Tehranian: All Muslims will agree on the following five items as constituting the fundamental doctrine of Islam, the so-called five pillars of Islam. They are:

- *Shahada* (profession): standing witness to Islam's truth by uttering, "There is no god but Allah, and Muhammad is His Prophet."
  Shi'a Muslims add to the phrase, "and Ali is his deputy". Ali was the Prophet's favorite cousin and son-in-law.
- *Salat* (prayer): praying five times a day facing Mecca at dawn, at noon, in the mid-afternoon, at dusk, and after dark.
- *Zakat* (charity): almsgiving to the poor.
- *Siyam* (fasting): fasting during the lunar month of Ramadan each day from sunrise to sunset by abstaining from food, drink, smoking, and sexual intercourse.
- *Haj* (pilgrimage): given the means, taking a pilgrimage to Mecca at least once in a lifetime.

Ikeda: So, those are the basic practices for Muslims.

If the religion of our time remained something personal—to heal one's psychological wounds—then it would be a kind of egotism and no more than a means of consolation or easing one's mind. If religious faith is used simply to work off corporate warriors' frustrations so they can devote themselves to the pursuit of profit once more, then our society won't change at all for the better.

In Islam, by contrast, faith is something a believer should practice in the context of daily life. There is a social aspect to it.

Tehranian: Exactly. And as we discussed earlier, that is also characteristic of Buddhism.

Ikeda: Of the five pillars you mentioned, the month of Ramadan and fasting during that period are particularly well known to us, too. You can't even drink a glass of water from sunrise to sunset. No matter how powerful or wealthy you may be, you cannot be exempt from this rule. Everyone is equally hungry.

Tehranian: The rule applies to everyone regardless of social status or wealth. There is perfect equality in order to cleanse the digestion system and to remind the rich of pangs of hunger.

Ikeda: Of course, sick or injured persons and pregnant women are not forced to abide by the rule. In that sense, the rule is not mandatory but observed spontaneously on the basis of one's faith.

Pilgrimage to Mecca, too, is not compulsory. As you said, "given the means" makes it more flexible, I suppose.

Tehranian: Yes, it does. By the way, have you ever been in an Islamic country during the month of Ramadan?

Ikeda: Yes, I have. My first visit to Iran was actually during Ramadan. From the point of view of workaholics like Japanese and Americans, it would seem to be an example of sheer inefficiency to try to work on an empty stomach during the daytime. But I think it is quite meaningful to have a "holy time" in one's daily life and to inject the "life of restraint" into a society controlled by the market economy where "desire" is given all-too-free rein.

When I visited Islamic countries during the month of Ramadan, I was afraid that people might be looking sour or extremely unfriendly, but actually the atmosphere I sensed was quite refreshing.

Tehranian: You become more conscious of your faith. Some people say they gain a sense of fulfillment. In daily life, in which we can easily become victim to inertia, Ramadan imparts a valuable sense of rhythm. I remember from the age of 15, the age of adulthood for Muslim boys, how eager I was to join the family in fasting. We would wake up just before sunrise to share a meal followed by morning prayers. There was a lot of excitement in the ritual.

Ikeda: Another familiar scene connected with Islam is the way believers offer prayers wherever they happen to be. Whether in a mosque, or in a modern office building, or on a college campus, Muslims—young and old, men and women—are seen praying, kneeling down on a carpet or rug.

Tehranian: They are praying in the direction of the Kaaba in Mecca. In Christianity or Buddhism, there are sanctuaries or chapels in which believers pray toward the object of worship placed in front of them. In Islam, however, even when you are in the mosque, you direct your prayer toward Mecca through the walls of the building. The reason for this practice is Islam's complete negation of icon worship, a major difference from other religions. You will find a hollow in the wall of any mosque in the direction of Mecca.

Ikeda: We often see in TV documentaries dealing with the Islamic world the scene of a mosque towering in the early morning mist and hear solemn sounds of *azan* chants coming out of the minarets: "Come for prayer!" "Come for prosperity!" "Praying is more wonderful than sleeping!" These words of *azan* chants heard in the morning left an indelible impression on my mind.

Let me ask you about one more thing here, and that is what do you say in your prayers?

Tehranian: We say, "God is great", and then "There is no God but God, and Muhammad is His Prophet", all in Arabic.

Ikeda: Those are the same words you utter when professing your faith. *Azan* chants and profession of faith are all said in Arabic, then?

Tehranian: That's right. Arabic is used throughout the world. We also greet each other by saying, "Salam Alaikum! (Peace be upon you!)".

Ikeda: As I recall it, you say "Salam Alaikum!" to people around you, looking to the left and then to the right, isn't that correct?

Tehranian: Yes. Symbolized in our prayer is a transcendental orientation whereby you face the sacred in a one-to-one relationship and a social orientation in which you look to others with warm-heartedness.

Ikeda: Speaking of prayers reminds me of an interesting episode. A Japanese woman, seeing her Muslim friend praying every day so many times, wondered what he was doing that for. She thought he probably had some big problem bothering him. Finally, she asked: "What are you asking God for? Success in the examinations?" His response was a reprimand: "You never ask God for a favor. That is not a prayer."

Tehranian: Prayer given in reverence to God and for peace of others is called "*salat*". It is not the same thing as supplication or asking a favor of God.

Supplication is not ruled out completely. Called *doa'a*, it is considered helpful in bringing humans closer to Allah. In any case, prayer is essentially for veneration of God and peace.

Ikeda: I see. What's so interesting about the episode I cited is that the Japanese often pray to some deity for success in entrance examinations or for happiness of their families at New Year's. The saying, "Man turns to God only when in trouble", applies perfectly to these people who forget prayer or god once the objective is achieved. New Year's visits to local shrines or temples, too, are usually more ceremonial or perfunctory than sincere, fervent prayers. In such a social milieu, those who pray daily are regarded as "weak persons who look to others for assistance".

In a society filled with such prejudices, the Soka Gakkai has been for many years carrying out a movement in which individual members offer daily prayers as a sincere demonstration of their faith.

Tehranian: I can see your point very well. Watchfulness that comes with prayers makes us aware of our own blessings and the needs of others.

Toward a Model of Multi-Civilizational Coexistence

Tehranian: After Prophet Muhammad's demise, the Ummayada empire came into power in 661 A.D., but it was replaced by the Abbasids in 750 A.D. The latter lasted for about 500 years.

During the reign of the Ummayads, Arab domination over non-Arab population was celebrated. The newly converted non-Arab people were severely discriminated against in terms of tax burden and social status. By contrast, the Abbasids made no distinction between the Arabs and non-Arabs; instead they emphasized whether or not a person believed in Allah and His messenger. Many non-Arabs—Persians, Turks, etc.—were welcomed into the government administration.

As you can see, the Islamic concept that all people are equal before Allah—and that is exactly the spirit of the Koranic message—was put into practice by the Abbasid empire.

Ikeda: I understand that some scholars classify the Ummayads as an Arab empire and the Abbasids as an Islamic empire. That seems to make sense.

I would now like to ask you how Islam under the Abbasids spread to other ethnic groups beyond the Arab population. It seems to me that Islam grew tremendously during the period of Abbasid rule because it became a universal religion not only conceptually but also as a historical movement.

Tehranian: Many tend to see Islam as a "religion of the desert" and an "Arab faith", but to show how widespread it is outside the Arab world, let me cite one simple figure: of about 1.4 billion Muslims today, only about 290 million are Arabs. Islam spread very rapidly in its first 100 years from the Arabian Peninsula into Asia, Africa, and Europe.

Ikeda: Those figures are ample evidence to refute the stereotyped images of Islam, for which Orientalism is to blame. To give another example, in France, the Catholic population is the largest, of course, but the second largest group is Muslim, not Protestant. We need to erase those fabricated images about Islam being a religion of the desert or of the Arabs only as soon as possible.

Tehranian: I agree. Islam could have easily taken the same route that some religions have historically taken as a "tribal" or "national" religion. It could have turned into a specifically Arab religion, but it did not.

Ikeda: That is exactly the point. How did it happen to be able to go beyond the confines of a tribe or race?

Tehranian: Islam became a universal religion because of several factors. First, the Koran makes it absolutely clear: "Verily, God makes no distinction among you except by your righteousness" (4.151).

Ikeda: You mean, in other words, the Koran itself is the source of Islam's universalism. Since it is based on divine revelation, the Koranic message is not simply a theory or an abstract principle, but the objective one should strive for.

Tehranian: Precisely. The second factor was the fact that the rapid expansion of Islam into the Persian and Byzantine empires brought it into contact with a vast number of different ethnic and religious groups.

Ikeda: Another popular image associated with Islam is that it expanded its sphere of influence by forcing other ethnic and/or religious groups to choose between "the sword or the Koran". But any authoritarian rule by power never lasts very long, even if it might seem successful for a short period of time. From what you have described, it is clear that interaction with a wide variety of ethnic groups and traditions made possible the diverse cultures of Islam.

Tehranian: That is right. The Abbasids built their empire on the principle of tolerance of cultural diversity. Earlier in our discussion we talked about the diversity of Islamic civilization, citing some concrete examples. Let me mention a few more episodes.

One of the great Aristotelian scholars, Ibn Rushd (Averroes), who exerted immense influence on medieval European theology, was a Muslim born in Cordoba, Spain. Cordoba is the birthplace of the Roman philosopher Seneca, the Christian priest-scholar Hosius, and the Jewish rabbi Maimonides, among others. Cordoba was a place where different civilizations interacted and mingled.

Ikeda: Cordoba was one of the three major cities of the Middle Ages, along with Constantinople and Baghdad.

Tehranian: There is a famous mosque in that city. When Spain was under Islamic rule, the mosque was used by Muslims on Fridays and by Christians on Sundays for their respective services.

Cordoba was also a commercial center where Jewish merchants were actively engaged in business. The place is indeed historical proof that different religions can not only exist side by side but can flourish together. And Cordoba was not an anomaly. There are many such examples. Sarajevo is a case in point.

Ikeda: Speaking of Sarajevo, Ivo Andric of the former Yugoslavia, winner of the Nobel Prize for literature (1961), wrote as follows in a letter of 1920:

> The dead of night in Sarajevo. The clock of the Catholic cathedral strikes two, with due solemnity. About a minute later, the Eastern Orthodox Church tells the time, faintly. A while afterward, the tower clock of the Islam temple makes a husky sound, indicating it is eleven Mecca time. The Jews, whose synagogue does not have any bell tower, live by their own time.

In former Yugoslavia, I was once told, Muslims presented a church to the local Catholics who were so poor that they could not afford to build one for themselves.

Tehranian: Andric's prose beautifully testifies to the coexistence of distinct elements as well as distinctions between coexisting elements. Many cities in Eurasia have similar characteristics.

Ikeda: Spanish writer Juan Goytisolo's *Sarajevo Notes* describes a more recent picture of the Balkan city, although much of the book is devoted to the tragedies that have taken place since the history of coexistence passed into oblivion.

Interviewed by a Japanese TV station, Goytisolo quietly talked about the religious diversity of Sarajevo. It is one of the largest Muslim cities in the Balkans, but the Spanish writer was struck by the way an Islamic mosque, Jewish synagogue and Greek Orthodox church were standing so close to each other.

On the level of ordinary people's daily lives, religious coexistence is possible. Sarajevo and many other cities in former Yugoslavia and elsewhere that are now torn apart by bloody religious conflict were until very recently models of religious coexistence. People of different faiths shared much with each other.

Focus on People's Daily Lives

Ikeda: Tsunesaburo Makiguchi, the founding president of Soka Gakkai and an outstanding geographer in his own right, points out in his major treatise, *A Geography of Human Life*, that maritime peoples are generally more open and more tolerant. That is because they usually have a long history of cross-cultural contact.

By extension, I believe cities built on desert oases are essentially similar to those of a maritime nation. The desert is equivalent to the ocean, and its oases are its ports, camels are its ships, and caravans are comparable to fleets sailing the seas.

Tehranian: Your analogy is very apt, and the image, I would say, is true to reality.

Ikeda: People of the oasis cities were in constant contact with other cultures and other ethnic groups. They welcomed such opportunities and benefited from them. Islam spread in Persia and Egypt through the established routes of transport connecting various oases ("ports") scattered here and there in the vast desert ("seas"). Insofar as Islam depended on and treasured these established routes, it had to take on the characteristics of cultural universality and diversity.

Tehranian: It is true, nonetheless, that Islam has also committed the sins of narrow-minded exclusiveness and intolerance. The early Arab conquerors often treated non-Muslims harshly.

Ikeda: Humans can be foolish and cruel at times, but they can also be wise and tolerant at others. People are often so weak that they commit crimes, but it is also people who perform magnificently noble acts. That is the wonder of being human.

Tehranian: We can thank history for showing us that nearly all nations have acted chivalrously at times and cruelly at other times.

Ikeda: Recognizing that, we must learn from history about the crucial importance of day-to-day contact and interchange. Be it in Sarajevo or Cordoba, people of different faiths used to live together peacefully.

Tehranian: Sometimes people forget an elementary fact of life that they can be driven by the group psychology of antagonism and hostility against each other.

Ikeda: Related to this theme of coexistence, I am very much fond of the hustle and bustle of the marketplace. By that, I do not mean the financial market where billions of dollars are transacted instantaneously, simply by typing in figures on a computer terminal. I'm talking about what is called in Persian a bazaar or in Arabic the *suq*. That is where life is; it symbolizes sharing and coexistence. There you find the friendly smiles of an old man and his wife who run a little mom-and-pop store. You meet total strangers who are generous and kind.

Tehranian: In 1992 such markets used to be anywhere and everywhere in the Isalmic world. I witnessed a lively bazaar in the outskirts of Ashkabad, Turkmenistan. By contrast, the government stores in the city were empty and dead.

Ikeda: I am not being nostalgic about the "good old days", nor am I indulging in the kind of exoticism that Edward Said criticized. All I am trying to say is that when you focus on the daily lives of people, you begin to see the possibility of coexistence between different cultures. Both Cordoba and Sarajevo, the cities we talked about, are rich reservoirs of human wisdom, from which we must learn a lesson about how different groups of people can live together.

Tehranian: That is precisely what we, members of the human race, must learn, or rather, must recall at this point in history.

The Human Factor

Ikeda: Modern times are said to have begun with the famous Cartesian proposition, "Cogito, ergo sum". "I think; therefore, I am". That is, human ideas and reason substantiate human existence; that somehow thinking takes precedence over being.

Tehranian: This was preceded by *Dubito, ergo cogito*, then *Cogito ergo sum*. Descartes declaration made it possible for human beings to doubt and think freely without being constrained. But the same freedom led humans to countless campaigns of slaughter on the pretext of defending some ideology or interest.

Ikeda: "Cogito, ergo sum", as I understand it, is the reverse of "Sum ergo, cogito", the statement of St. Thomas Aquinas, that greatest of medieval Christian philosophers, who was deeply influenced by Islamic philosophy. "Sum ergo, cogito", it seems to me, bespeaks the gravity of real life. "I am". "You are". These declarations testify to the irrefutable value of living.

Any idea, philosophy, or religion is one-sided if it is removed from the realities of human beings, human life, and day-to-day living. It is high time now to reinstate the actual weight of human life in all fields—science and technology, economics, medicine, politics, and so forth.

Tehranian: It is safe, perhaps, to say that Islam flourished, especially during the Abbasid period, because it showed enough concern for actual living and real people. *Zakat* originally meant paying back debts to Allah, but in actuality the money is used to help orphans, widows, and the poor. The underlying spirit here seeks to realize the ideal world on earth, while continuing the quest for the divine.

Ikeda: Although Buddhism is not a monotheistic religion, there is a similar idea in its teachings: "Bodhisattvas elevate themselves on the one hand, but on the other, they descend to the level of the unenlightened to save them." In other words, Bodhisattvas, while aiming at the attainment of enlightenment, endeavor to improve the conditions of actual society as the locus of the manifestation of Buddha wisdom.

Tehranian: In a beautiful poem entitled "Conference of the Birds", the 12th-century Sufi poet Farid ad-Din Attar provides a suggestive allegory to recount the joys and hardships of man's spiritual journey. As I mentioned earlier, Sufism was greatly influenced by Buddhism.

Ikeda: Attar is said to have taught Rùmi, that great Sufi poet and thinker. I would be interested in hearing the story. Please tell us about the poem.

Tehranian: All the birds of the world assemble at a conference to discuss the whereabouts of their mythical god, Simurgh (the Phoenix). Hudhud (the Hoopoe) leads them in their discussion revealing that he knows where Simurgh lives in the high mountains. In order to find him, the birds follow Hudhud on a long journey. This takes them through seven valleys named after the stages of the Sufi spiritual path of development.

Ikeda: The search for the truth turns into a tale of adventure, an important aspect of Islamic civilization centered on interchange and trade. What are the seven valleys?

Tehranian: The birds continue their journey from Search to Love, Knowledge, Amazement, Contentment, Riches, and Poverty. Along the way, many birds drift off course for one reason or another, making excuses, being distracted, or falling behind.

Ikeda: An intriguing story, indeed. Birds drop out for a variety of reasons. It shows the poet's deep insight into the diversity of humanity.

Tehranian: When they reach the peak of the mountain where Simurgh is supposed to be lodged, only thirty birds are left. They look around …

Ikeda: And nowhere is Simurgh to be found …

Tehranian: That is right. The birds look around and discover themselves, Simurgh. In Persian, Simurgh also means thirty birds. This is a clever play on words, but by this allegory, Attar is teaching us that divinity lies in the interdependence and community of all life forms. We are, therefore I am.

Ikeda: A similar allegory can probably be found in Buddhist tales as well. An ideal is not something up there or over there beyond our reach; it is in the very process of seeking an ideal. Buddhism teaches that the *saha* world is the Land of Eternally Tranquil Light. This world is full of suffering, but the way people endure such suffering is itself the way of the Buddha.

Buddhism also has the idea that earthly desire equals enlightenment. The absence of suffering does not necessarily mean happiness. The nobility of being human lies in squarely confronting this suffering.

Tehranian: I see. How to reconcile religious faith and actual society—we must begin by understanding what the allegory teaches us and the Buddhist philosophy you just explained to me.

Ikeda: I agree with you completely. In one of the poems in *Gitanjali* (1912), the great Bengali poet Rabindranath Tagore sang as follows:

Leave this chanting and singing and telling of beads!
Whom dost thou worship in this lonely dark corner of a temple with doors all shut?

Open thine eyes and see thy God is not before thee!
He is there where the tiller is tilling the hard ground
and where the pathmaker is breaking stones.
He is with them in sun and in shower,
and his garment is covered with dust.
Put off thy holy mantle and even like him come down on the dusty soil!

What I see in this poem is the perfect harmony between modern humanism and religious faith. The Way of the Bodhisattva in Mahayana Buddhism is of the same spirit.

Tehranian: That is right. Secular modernity and religious faith are not mutually exclusive. On the contrary, without such a religious faith, the future of modernity is bleak.

Ikeda: Mahatma Gandhi said the same thing. Sad as it is, the history of the 20th century has proved it to be correct.

Tehranian: Yes. The modern world without the moral and spiritual guidance of major religions can destroy itself through pollution, over-population, nuclear, biological, and chemical war, or a slow death in spiritual and moral poverty.

Ikeda: One of the first scientists to warn against the environmental crisis of our time, Rachael Carson used the phrase "a sense of wonder". I interpret this phrase to mean "a sense of awe" *vis-à-vis* others and the unknown. It is this sense that is missing in our time. Everything is considered predictable, nothing is thought to be unknown or unfathomable. Humans are believed capable of controlling and processing everything.

Tehranian: That is precisely the hubris of secular humanism. But humanism does not address the great mysteries of human destiny, i.e. our finitude, fragility, and moral frailty. Religious faith does. That is why it awes, attracts, and mystifies.

Ikeda: Instead of being contemptuous of or hostile to others, we must look at everything around us with a sense of wonder and a sense of awe. Then you feel the "gravity of existence" and the "weight of life". To keep such a sense always alive and fresh, religious sensitivity to that which is eternal and that which transcends us is absolutely necessary.

Tehranian: I find myself in full agreement with you.

CHAPTER 5

Spiritual and Religious Revivals

Ikeda: As I have repeatedly pointed out in this series of discussions, the religious spirit has been steadily waning in our time, especially among young people. I wonder if the same is true in Islamic countries.

Tehranian: Well, I would say that if anything, young people are more seriously interested in studying the Islamic doctrine and observing religious traditions than the older generations.

But ironically in Iran, where the clerics are in power, people are increasingly critical of the abuse of religious power for political purposes.

Ikeda: I was once told that quite a few young Muslims who have studied in Europe or the United States came home disenchanted with modern civilization and reverted to their Islamic traditions.

In Japan and the West, the religious spirit is clearly drying up, so to speak. In parallel with it, an increasing number of young people are being attracted by the occult and by superstition.

Tehranian: That's quite true. Ironic as it may be, popular belief in magic and superstition seems to be growing in pace with the progress of science. It seems to me that while confidence in religious institutions is declining, the hunger for spirituality is growing.

Ikeda: Scientific and technological development was supposed to dispel the darkness of human ignorance and bring about a bright future, but where has it led us? The light is of napalm bombs and the flash of atomic bombs, and it has dispelled not the darkness of human ignorance but the lives of countless millions of innocent people. The evil flash of mass destruction, rather than the light of hope that illuminates everything in the world—this is nothing but the darkness of violence carried to the extreme.

Tehranian: The tragedy of the 20th century, indeed. As violence grows, the human spirit feels more homeless.

Ikeda: Originally, technology was a tool with which to create things of value, but it has ended up producing the atomic bomb and consuming huge amounts of data, giving birth to the mass information society.

Tehranian: Television is certainly an example of the information-consuming technology that you're talking about. We have access to a massive amount of information through television and computers. Yet, it is doubtful that such information has led us to a more informed and meaningful way of life. All too often, we use technology and tools of modern convenience simply to consume more and more fragmented information.

Ikeda: Technology is now being used to *consume*, rather than to *produce*. We even consume technology itself.

Tehranian: Both tools and technology are improved and upgraded all the time these days, and that drives people to buy new models before they've really used the old ones. Technological society appears to be a beast that is consuming itself.

Ikeda: To consume something is to reduce its value. A brand new thing you've just purchased is perhaps worth the price you paid for it, and if it's a new model, its value increases to the extent you feel proud to possess it. But once a thing gets old or everyone else has the same model, the value of your possession diminishes and you want to buy something new and more valuable. This pattern of consumption does not give one the joy of creating new value.

The religious spirit is completely the opposite. We could call it a "value-creating soul". To me, the religious spirit is a state of mind that shares a sense of solidarity with even an ordinary stone on the roadside. It is the spirit that truly aspires to the well being of people at the opposite ends of the globe whom one might never meet.

Tehranian: As you have pointed out, the human spirit creates increasing value, but consumption of objects leads to diminishing value. The same can be said of love and knowledge. The more you love, the more love you gain. The more knowledge you share, the more knowledgeable you become.

Ikeda: Put another way, the religious spirit is a kind of mental capacity that turns nihilism into a bright future and despair into hope. A cynic sees everything as empty or worthless, and the soul of such a person will not create anything of value. Science has brought light to our external world, but our inner world still remains dark. Is it not philosophy or what I call "the religious spirit" that will brighten our inner world?

Tehranian: I believe so. By "religious spirit", you don't mean faith in a particular religion or a set of particular rituals and institution, but rather a more general state of mind, an attitude toward life. Right?

Ikeda: Yes, that is right. Unfortunately, however, the religious spirit is definitely on the decline in our time. How should we cope with this dangerous development? Fortunately, we can look to history for a prescription.

Tehranian: Buddhism and Islam certainly offer their prescriptions, as we have discussed. They both began as movements for spiritual liberation of the masses from superstition.

Ikeda: Of course, we are not talking about any particular religious doctrine. As I understand it, the word Islam means "active submission to God". I think that is basically in line with Paul Tillich's (1886–1965) definition of religion as "concern with the ultimate ground of being".

Tehranian: Very true. Islam means active and full participation in and compassion for being in all of its forms. It means active peace, a condition that combines love with courage.

Ikeda: Earlier, we also talked about Islam being a "religious reform movement". By demanding "active submission", Muhammad expressed his criticism of the tribal magical religions and his skepticism of the Judaism and Christianity of his day. Is that correct?

Tehranian: Yes. "We [Muslims] look to Him [Allah] alone" (II. 139)—these words in the Koran testify to Muhammad's skepticism of Judaism and Christianity. He was also thoroughly critical of tribal polytheism.

By the way, your mention of Tillich reminds me of my days at Harvard when I took his courses. He was a great teacher. I learned much from him about religious spirit that is common to all great spiritual traditions.

Ikeda: I know. Tillich went into exile when the Nazis took over and sought refuge in the United States. He was teaching at Harvard when you were a student there. You are really lucky to have studied under such a great scholar.

Tehranian: I think so, too. Your mentor, Josei Toda, was a gifted teacher, too. It is really a wonderful thing to have outstanding people as one's mentors.

Ikeda: Tillich's book *The Courage To Be* (1952) has given hope to those of us who lived after Auschwitz and Hiroshima. It is an immortal work, a great asset to humankind.

Tehranian: Right. In the book, Tillich squarely confronts the agony and despair of our time, and appeals, "Let us live on notwithstanding!"

Ikeda: "*Notwithstanding*"—*trotz* in German—is the key word in *The Courage To Be*. It is comparable to Viktor E. Frankl's *Ein Psycholog erlebt das Konzentrationslager* (1947), the masterpiece of the century, in that the Austrian psychoanalyst declares, "Let's still say yes to life!"

Tehranian: As a survivor of Auschwitz, Frankl had seen the worst aspects of human nature, and yet he was willing to trust humanity and take a positive view of life.

Ikeda: Frankl's attitude is akin to "pessimism of the intellect and optimism of the will", Antonio Gramsci's famous phrase, which Edward Said made his motto.

"Optimism of the will" could be paraphrased as "courage never to yield". Persons with such courage never avert their gaze from the dark side of reality and yet never stop marching forward.

Tehranian: I agree with you completely but, I'd like to add, "compassion of the heart" to Gramsci's motto. Buddhists, Christians, and Muslims have done so in their faith. Those people all have the same orientation, the same stance. Fundamentally, they look into the abyss of death and despair while turning to life and hope. In Hawaiian tradition, there are two guideposts that one should follow in life: *aloha* and *kupono*. *Aloha* is the equivalent of love and *kupono* is the equivalent of courage, i.e. standing for what you believe is right.

Ikeda: "Optimism of the will" is miles away from the frivolous kind of optimism with which some people are preoccupied in satisfying their desires and seeking pleasure without even looking at the abyss of reality.

We cannot just blame Hitler and the Nazis for the great miseries of humankind in this century. Tillich spoke of the possibility of democracy degenerating into complacency, and being swallowed up by cynicism, apathy, and the inertia of nihilism.

Tillich's message in *The Courage To Be* is the need for a strong will-power to live on despite the darkness lurking in the depths of human existence.

Tehranian: When I was a graduate student at Harvard, I often audited Professor Tillich's lectures. His understanding of religion as "concern with the ultimate ground of being" is close to my own understanding. His definition of religion applies perfectly to Islam.

The Koran uses the phrase, "al-din al-gavim", meaning "an eternally immutable religion" to express its universality.

Ikeda: I'd also like to add that Muhammad's admonition to "return to Abraham's time" was not a fundamentalist call for reversion to the original source of faith, but a search for "the religious", something more universal than a specific religion.

Tehranian: In your second lecture at Harvard, "Mahayana Buddhism and Twenty-first-century Civilization" (1993), you discussed the importance of "that which is religious". "The religious" and the religious spirit that you've been talking about are like two sides of the same coin.

Ikeda: In Buddhism, there is the term "The Buddha's mother", which refers to Dharma, among other things. It is the fundamental teaching from which Buddhas are born. This concept testifies to the Buddhist concern for the universal, the ultimate.

"Concern for the ultimate" may sound fanatical or exclusivistic, but exclusive fanaticism can never be "ultimate". Fanatics are parochial and irrational, and their concern is not with "the ground of human existence" but with personal objectives and self-interest. At times, fanaticism serves as the driving force for nationalistic fervor.

"Concern" means one's search for the source of human existence with all the goodness and the power of good inherent in human nature. Seeking answers to questions like "What is a human being?" and "What was I born for?" can never be exclusivistic. I would say that "concern for the ultimate" is essentially a humanistic concern.

Tehranian: But as you have said many times, humanism should not limit itself just to humans. Humanism should concern itself with all the ground of human life, including all creatures small or big. The error of the European Enlightenment was that it put humans above nature.

Prophet and Fortune-teller

Ikeda: We may be digressing a bit from the main subject of our discussion, but prophets appear in Jewish, Christian, and Islamic scriptures. In Japan, however, since the words for prophet and fortune-teller are pronounced exactly the same, people often think that a prophet has the supernatural power with which to predict the future. Many mistakenly believe that prophets are fortune-tellers.

Tehranian: Generally speaking, we often use the same terms, but with entirely different meanings in mind. We are thus all hostage to our languages. That is why a method of discourse that takes language only as a point of departure and tries to deconstruct the meanings behind words is a good method for dialogue and mutual understanding.

Ikeda: I am of the same opinion. When someone uses the word prophet, for example, we must be careful to see in what context it is being used and form our judgment on that basis. People too often jump at an arbitrary judgment on the basis of their preconceptions without going to the extra trouble of trying to understand the specific context of a statement.

Looking at Buddhist traditions, we find both Shakyamuni and the Mahayana scholar Nagarjuna took great care in using their language. They kept showing their contemporaries how deceptive linguistic habits and prevailing notions could be.

Tehranian: I see your point very well.

Ikeda: Buddhism differentiates between wording, meaning, and intent. Wording stands for a literal or superficial meaning of a statement. Meaning takes into account the syntax and context necessary for understanding what a word or sentence signifies. Intent refers to the consciousness of the writer who used the word or sentence. In terms of the Buddhist sutras, intent means the spirit of the Buddha.

Of the three, intent is the most important; it makes a big difference whether the word or statement is motivated by the malicious intent to deceive or control other people or by a genuine wish for their well-being.

When Japanese confuse prophet and fortune-teller just because their pronunciations are the same, they have not even passed the first stage of grasping the literal meaning of a word or sentence.

Tehranian: In religion in general, a prophet is related to what is called mysticism in the science of religion. Mysticism is quite different from occultism; in principle it attaches greater importance to experience than to doctrine. There are great mysteries in the universe such as the beginning and end of cosmos and life. Mysticism acknowledges these mysteries but instead of trying to explain them, it accepts them in awe and admiration.

Ikeda: The word "mystic" often evokes an image of a miracle or some supernatural phenomenon or power. But Safl Ibn Abdillah, the well-known Muslim mystic, says, "The greatest miracle is to change the bad character into a good one."

Tehranian: Right. Mysticism is focused on experience rather than miracles. It follows the spirit rather than the letter of the law.

Ikeda: Scriptures, of course, are indispensable; they are the point of departure in any major religion. But over time, scholars and theologians provide their interpretations and annotations of the scriptural message, and soon the interpreters become more authoritative than the original. In the process, the intent of the writers is often forgotten.

When that happens, prophets sometimes appear, criticizing the past religious literature, established doctrines, and corrupt clergy and ecclesiastical authorities. Based on their personal religious experience, these prophets convey the intent of God's word in an attempt to restore the religious spirit among the faithful. This has happened in many religions over and over again.

Tehranian: That is true. In Zoroastrianism, there is even a prophecy that every thousand years a new prophet will appear to guide humanity. That is why in the legend the three Zoroastrian *magi* (priests) were looking for baby Jesus by following the stars.

Ikeda: The advent of prophets and their warnings are significant, but mysticism could degenerate into arbitrariness. With the end of the century just behind us, we have seen several self-appointed "prophets" or "fortune-tellers" appear, making pronouncements or predictions that misguide the masses and kindle unnecessary anxiety among them.

Tehranian: Exactly. That's why we need a reliable set of criteria to judge the authenticity of prophecies.

Ikeda: That's right.

Tehranian: What should be the criteria, then?

Ikeda: If we look at those movements in history that led to major reforms or reformations, we find prophets urging people to "return to the original teaching" rather than making arbitrary predictions. Martin Luther was such a prophet. Nichiren Daishonin, too, called for "return to the spirit of the Lotus Sutra!" His intent was to free the spirit of the original scripture from the rigid interpretations of Buddhist scholars.

"Practice as the Buddha taught", another important phrase in Buddhism, was Nichiren's criterion in going beyond arbitrariness to achieve universality for his prophecy. In other words, the proximity of his experience with that of Shakyamuni was the yardstick.

Tehranian: Islam considers itself a recurring but eternal message conveyed to humanity through God's prophets. A prophet is therefore not a fortune-teller. He is God's chosen channel to warn and promise humanity about the consequences of their actions. Muhammad considered himself a mere mortal who is only conveying God's eternal message translated through prophets from Adam to Noah, Moses, and Jesus.

Ikeda: That's probably the reason why prophets were often rejected in their native land. Because of their warnings, they were persecuted by those in power and subjected to popular contempt and disregard.

People can immerse themselves in self-reflection in the midst of deep prayers. Absorbed in fervent prayer, people may think about the plight of others in distress and shed tears. On the verge of feeling overcome by various difficulties, one can regain courage through intense prayer. This is what religion is. This is what prayer is, and this is faith. Any country that looks down on religious faith is spiritually impoverished, I must say. It is precisely in such a country that we find established religions degenerating into self-serving egotism and people bewitched by occultism and superstition.

Tehranian: It was such a sense of crisis that led Muhammad, as well as the Buddha and Jesus, to criticize and issue warnings. Martin Luther also falls in this category.

Ikeda: Nichiren Buddhism, too, began in the same way. Nichiren Daishonin squarely confronted the established religions of his day that had become aristocratic and contemptuous of the ordinary folk and degenerated into formalistic and ritualistic observances.

Our Soka Gakkai, too, began as a religious reform movement aimed at revitalizing a Buddhism that had been transformed into a ceremonial religion (a religion for funeral and memorial services) from the time of the Tokugawa shogunate. Our motto has been "Return to Shakyamuni's spirit and to the founding spirit of Nichiren Daishonin!"

Activating the Community of Spirit

Ikeda: History is one thing; now, I would like us to take up the question of what the two religions can contribute to contemporary society, that is, the significance of Islam and Buddhism in our time.

Tehranian: Let us do so by all means.

Ikeda: We live in an era characterized by "division and confrontation". All sorts of ideologies, views, and even hobbies and personal preferences differentiate people. These differences are not necessarily the mark of individuality, however. More often than not, they seem to have been fabricated to strengthen people's sense of belonging to or identity with rigidly standardized groups.

Tehranian: I think that's very true. Rapid mobility leads to psychological dislocation. Dislocation leads to identity anxiety. Anxiety leads to fetishism. Fetishism latches on to consumer commodities or identities to gain a sense of false security. For instance, Orientalism plays up the conflict between East and West. The myth of capitalism vs. communism provided an identity fetish during the Cold War. These stereotyped images have made open and candid exchange of views—dialogue—very difficult.

Ikeda: What I'd like to bring up here is the possibility of a community in which people can gather together without excluding anyone. The Islamic term for community is *umma*, and the Buddhist equivalent is *samgha*.

Tehranian: That's a big subject. The first thing that comes to mind is the etymology of the word "religion". In English the word suggests "to tie, to fasten, to bind".

Ikeda: In Judaism, Christianity, and Islam, each individual is "tied" with God, right?

Tehranian: In the Abrahamic traditions, Jews, Christians, and Muslims have entered into a covenant with God to live righteously. In Arabic, *mithaq* is the word for covenant.

In Islam, this covenant is fortified by the utterance of *shahada* (witness): "There is no God but God, and Muhammad is His Prophet." By uttering the *shahada*, anyone regardless of gender, race, religion, or ethnic group could become a Muslim. Once the first Islamic state was established in Medina, anyone could also enter into covenant (*bay'a*) with the Prophet to come under the protection of the new state. That is how the Islamic *umma* was first established.

A passage in the Koran says:

> And there may spring from you a nation who invites to goodness, and enjoins right conduct and forbids indecency. Such are they who are successful. (3.104)

The formation of the *umma* in Medina could be that it was time for the relationship between God and a small number of individuals established in Mecca to develop into a dynamic social relationship among the people.

Ikeda: It was time for the faithful themselves to realize in society such attributes of God as mercy, generosity, and truthfulness, wasn't it? And the *umma* was to provide a base for such social life.

Tehranian: That is correct. The *umma* is not a religious group isolated from society but rather society itself of people who share the same faith. Every chapter in the Koran begins with the ringing phrase, "In the Name of Allah, the Compassionate and the Merciful." Those who accuse Islam as the religion of the sword don't know what they are talking about.

Ikeda: With the formation of the *umma*, Islam became a communal organization based on faith. Up until then, the tribal community had been cemented by blood relationship.

Tehranian: One of his opponents accused Muhammad of severing the bond of blood. Blood relationship had been that strong, unquestioned. By contrast, the principle consolidating the *umma* was "faith".

Ikeda: A community based on blood ties may be solid, but it is by nature closed, and as such it can breed discrimination and oppression.

Tehranian: "Like the teeth of a comb in the hands of a weaver, all men are equal. White men cannot have a sense of their own superiority to black men." This is an oral tradition attributed to Muhammad.

An Islamic community was not composed of Muslims alone. Called "*dhimmis*", people of other faiths were able to maintain themselves within the "house of Islam".

Ikeda: The Buddhist community, too, was not a closed group but served as a bridge between Buddhist principles and social realities. The *samgha*, the community of early Buddhism, meant a gathering, congregation, and a guild.

Tehranian: Was the *samgha* something that had existed in Indian society or something originally created by Buddhism?

Ikeda: Shakyamuni applied a model that had existed in Indian society to the Buddhist community.

In those days, rice cultivation led to the emergence of the polis and economic activity was growing. Some of those city-states had adopted a democratic republican system. Their economic activity was centered around the guild-like community. The republican system and guild-like community were called *samgha*.

Tehranian: The Buddha, then, found a model for his religious community in the democratic republican system that was existing in society. That's very intriguing, indeed.

Ikeda: That's right. *Samgha* was an ideal human group for Shakyamuni.

Tehranian: I can see some basic similarities with the *umma*.

Ikeda: This Buddhist community encouraged the practice of four ways of leading sentient beings to emancipation.
They were:

• almsgiving, spiritual and material;
• loving speech;
• benefiting sentient beings with good conduct of body, speech, and mind;
• assuming the same form as that of the various sentient beings to be benefited.

Tehranian: They are all very specific and practical indices of conduct.

Ikeda: Yes, indeed. The *samgha* was the locus of activity for putting the Buddhist teachings into practice in society.
In any case, since any genuine religion must address itself to self-discipline and salvation of others, it is only natural that it should present a model for society by forming an ideal community of the faithful.

Tehranian: I agree. That's precisely the *umma*'s ideal, too. However, ideals often fall short of realities because of our human failures. The two wars that took place in the Persian Gulf in 1980–88 and 1991 pitted Muslims against Muslims.

Ikeda: During Japan's medieval period, there was a certain high priest who was so aloof that he did not even know about the ongoing civil war between the Taira (Heike) and Minamoto (Genji) clans. For a priest, it may be necessary at least for a period of time to shun all involvement in the realities to lead an ascetic life. But a high priest is the leader of a religious order, and as such he should know what is going on in secular society. If he does not, that means that his monastic order is a closed group. Shakyamuni himself taught his disciples to travel around the country as itinerant priests to help bring happiness to the people.

An organization is a pivotal point at which ideals and realities interact. A lively organization can help change reality toward an ideal, while at the same time interaction with reality through an organization prevents an ideal from becoming a narrow dogma.

Tehranian: Unfortunate as it is, though, individualism has gone too far in recent years, and with it the tendency to avert organizational affiliation has been growing. Fortunately, Islamic countries meet periodically in an organization called Conference of Islamic States.

Ikeda: Groups based on exclusion deserve to be criticized. We must closely examine a given organization in terms of its professed ideals and the kind of contribution it is making to society.

There are all sorts of human groups, including the family. If we rejected organizations completely, we would end up with the state apparatus alone growing "hypertrophied". In fact, the 20th century has witnessed many examples of the state becoming all too powerful.

Behind the current tendency of aversion to organizational affiliation, I cannot but see the twin swelling of egotism and statism. What we need now is to build a network of solidarity among people across the boundaries of nation-states.

Tehranian: I believe so, too. Dialogue is the method for building such a network. Toda Institute has now an International Advisory Council of over 400 prominent world citizens and growing.

Ikeda: Dialogue is "blood" for an organization to carry nutrients and oxygen through its body and keep it alive. The presence or absence of such blood determines life or death of an organization.

On Views of Equality

Ikeda: For an ideal community and genuine organization, equality is one of the essential conditions. Members must have a firm view of equality.

Nichiren once called the most powerful leaders of his time "the rulers of this little island country" (*Selected Writings of Nichiren*, Columbia University Press. New York, 1990, p. 322). He knew exactly what they were—petty beings completely in the dark about the world.

The Daishonin described himself as one "who was born poor and lowly to a *candala* family … Since my heart believes in the Lotus Sutra, I do not fear even *Bonten* or *Taishaku*, …" (*Letters of Nichiren*, Columbia University Press, New York, 1996, p. 56). *Candala* is a general name for outcasts who engage in professions considered menial or unclean and Bonten and Taishaku are considered gods.

By identifying himself with people who were most severely discriminated against, the Daishonin proclaimed the "nobility of the soul" by virtue of faith in the Lotus Sutra from the vantage point of a man at the bottom of society.

The Daishonin also proclaimed the essential equality of gender by saying, "There should be no discrimination among [people] … be they men or women" (*Letters of Nichiren*, p. 361).

Tehranian: For modern people, those words are nothing spectacular. The Japan of the 13th century was totally different, however. Uttering such words must have meant persecution.

Ikeda: The uniqueness of the Buddhist view of equality lies in seeing Buddha nature in each and every person. It does not derive from pity for those discriminated against but is based on respect for the Buddha nature equally inherent in human beings.

Chapter 20 of the Lotus Sutra, "The Bodhisattva Never Disparaging", describes how the bodhisattva always held all the people he met in reverence, worshipping them in respect for their Buddha nature. The Sanskrit word for worship is *namas kara* or *namas te*. They both mean "I respect you".

Tehranian: Even today people in India and Nepal say "*namas te*" in their greetings. The Indian greeting by clasping the two hands together and bowing is a symbol of praying to the divine in each other.

Ikeda: Most likely the expression derives from the same tradition.

To recapitulate, the basis of the Buddhist concept of equality is respect for other people. If you want to help others in distress because you are superior to them and more blessed than they are, then your kindness is tainted by egotism.

Altruistic acts must be rooted in profound respect for the Buddha nature of the person you are helping. You must think you are serving the Buddha nature, and that way you can prevent altruism from lapsing into hypocrisy.

Tehranian: Those are truly admirable words. I shall engrave your words in my heart.

We have already covered a lot of ground about the Islamic view of equality, but for the sake of comparison with the Buddhist view, let me go back to this point.

Islam appeared on the historical scene at a time (622 A.D.) when Arabia as well as the Persian (Sassanid, 226–651 A.D.) and Byzantine Empires in West Asia were characterized by enormous social inequities resembling the caste system.

Ikeda: Mecca, situated in the periphery of the major empires of West Asia and Europe, had become a thriving trade center between South and West Asia. In the meantime, however, destitution in the midst of affluence was growing and economic disparities were widening.

Tehranian: As usual, prosperity had to be an exacerbation of inequities. As we have seen, Muhammad's messages of monotheism and human equality soon gained him a following as well as the wrath of his own tribe, the Qureish. He and his disciples had to flee from Mecca to Medina. The first Islamic state in Medina established the rules of equality among Muslims and non-Muslims.

Ikeda: You mean the Medina Constitution.

Tehranian: Yes. All Muslims were declared equal in the sight of God except for what distinguished them in piety.

Ikeda: If they paid taxes, non-Muslims were entitled to self-rule as *dhimmis*, weren't they?

Tehranian: Yes. Their autonomous communities came under the protection of the Islamic state. At the time, slavery and female infanticide were prevailing practices in Arabia. Islam strictly prohibited infanticide, and slaves could become free by accepting Islam. Freeing of slaves became an act of Muslim piety.

Ikeda: Few of us have ever heard of Islam being responsible for the freeing of slaves.

Tehranian: Women and orphans suffered from enormous disadvantage in those days. Islam regulated family relations in great detail in order to protect the rights of children. By contemporary standards, some Islamic laws of marriage, divorce, and inheritance maintain inequity among men and women but Islamic societies are trying to change them.

Ikeda: Since Muhammad lost his parents in his early childhood, he set forth rules for the generous protection of orphans and others living in destitution.

In pre-Islamic tribal societies, the right to inheritance had been limited to males on the paternal side. Muhammad gave the right to women and orphans as well.

Tehranian: The notorious Koranic injunction that men are allowed to marry four wives, provided they could maintain justice among them, could be interpreted as a way to help protect the widows and orphans who had lost their husbands or fathers in wars.

Muhammad had also established rules of coexistence between Muslims and non-Muslims far ahead of the levels of political and religious tolerance at his time. Islam, therefore, represented a progressive system for its own time.

Ikeda: You mean the guarantee of safety for non-Muslims as *dhimmis* provided in the Medina Constitution. The fact that the minorities were duly incorporated in the legal system is highly commendable.

Tehranian: Some European and American historians have argued that the traditional Islamic societies showed a higher level of equality and tolerance than the traditional Christian West.

Ikeda: The historian Mark Cohen, for example, concluded through his comparison of the medieval Islamic societies and persecution of the Jews in Europe that *dhimmis* were protected, rather than persecuted, even though there were some inequities in the tax system.

Tehranian: The *millet* system under the Ottoman Empire, for instance, allowed a level of autonomy among the religious minorities that some persecuted Christian minorities did not enjoy in Christendom. Following the Arab-Israeli conflicts, however, the position of Jews in Islamic countries has become precarious. In some countries, such as Iran and Sudan, Baha'ians and Christians are also persecuted.

Ikeda: Jews, for example, formed their own communities, in which they were able to maintain their cultural traditions.

Equality should not mean sameness. We must recognize the differences but should not discriminate because of such differences. Eliminating the difference is not equality at all.

Tehranian: The tendency in modern mass societies is to measure everyone with the same yardstick, and that is not just. Intelligence tests (IQ tests) are a clear example of this. By developing standardized tests which measure the verbal and mathematical aptitudes, other types of intelligence such as physical dexterity, musical aptitude, and social skills have been severely undervalued.

Ikeda: Exactly. IQ tests can never measure the level of considerateness for others or one's courage in fighting against evil. And yet these spiritual qualities are the greatest of human virtues.

Tehranian: Justice and equality require that we begin with the assumption of human diversity while celebrating its value.

A society best serves the cause of equality and justice that makes the fulfillment of the different potentials of each the condition for the fulfillment of potentials of all. Gender, racial, ethnic or age differences must be celebrated and respected instead of being used as a basis for discrimination.

Ikeda: Differences should be a basis for respect, not for discrimination—that's really a splendid idea. I agree fully.

The Buddhist view that goes by the key words "cherry, plum, peach, and apricot" is also an endorsement of individuality and diversity. Each kind of tree has its own merit and values.

By letting each person display his/her individuality fully, society itself can benefit from the richness and fruits of diversity.

Tehranian: That's perfectly true.

CHAPTER 6

Clash of Civilizations

Ikeda: In December, 1998 the United States and Great Britain targetted Iraq for bombing.

Tehranian: As I see it, we shouldn't single out just Iraq as an isolated problem. It is high time now for all the countries concerned to get together and devise ways to establish the common security of the Persian Gulf area as a whole from a long-range perspective.

The eight Gulf states and the five permanent members of the UN Security Council should meet for thoroughgoing deliberations on all the pertinent issues.

Ikeda: Of urgent necessity is a comprehensive, multidimensional vision for the region, which should include plans for arms reduction aimed at easing the overall tension and for regional economic cooperation. I would very much like to see the Toda Institute address the problem and come up with concrete proposals.

Tehranian: As a matter of fact, the Institute has been sponsoring a "West Asian Security Forum" held in Istanbul in 1999, Cyprus in 2000, Doha in 2001, and Cyprus again in 2002. We approached the whole issue in a fundamental way and worked out a new set of proposals toward a comprehensive solution. The senior diplomats and scholars who attended these meetings now constitute a core of peacemakers in the region.

Ikeda: Well, it's a very timely and vitally important initiative. I wish you much success! At the time of the Gulf War in January, 1991, you composed a poem expressing your view on the war, and your daughter Maryam, then 16, wrote a poem in response to yours. It was, indeed, a beautiful exchange between father and daughter. Your poem reads, in part,

Wars
conjure up demons in us!
. . . . . .
My demons
. . . . . .
Lashing out at you
with my red,
poisonous tongue
and cold spears of anger to devour
all your humanity
with my boundless greed and vanity.

In his historic speech of September 8, 1957 calling for a ban on atomic and hydrogen bombs, Josei Toda also talked about the Devil. "We, the people of the world", he declared, "all have the right to life. Anything that threatens our right to existence is a Devil, a Satan, a Monster!" Your verse very much echoes the cries of my mentor.

Tehranian: I have enormous admiration for the first three presidents of the Soka Gakkai. They each had tremendous personal difficulties to surmount, yet devoted their lives to the benefit of humankind. Through their courageous action they created beautiful, noble values. Countless people suffer in this world, but only a small number can ever reorient their lives toward the noble cause of fighting for humanity.

Ikeda: To overcome personal struggles and transform oneself into a new person who can contribute to the well being of humankind—this is our ideal of "human revolution". It is also the starting point for our movement for world peace.

The Toda Institute was established to lay the foundations for guiding humanity toward happiness. There is perhaps nothing sensational about its work, but the important thing is to keep pursuing the lofty ideal—like the dashing of waves upon rocks. Returning in countless waves, the water rounds off the rough and cruel edges of the rocks. A person who makes this kind of untiring effort is truly a "champion" among human beings. Up until now, we have been talking about Buddhism and Islam. Now, let's focus our discussion on "open dialogue" between civilizations.

Views on Civilization—Toynbee and Others

Ikeda: The word "civilization" reminds us of theories advanced by people like Oswald Spengler and Arnold Toynbee. In their bird's-eye views of human history, they both employed the concept of the "rise and fall" of civilizations, although their theses were miles apart.

In his *Decline of the West*, Spengler assumed that each civilization was self-contained and complete in itself, isolated from all others. All underwent the same process, beginning with "birth" and culminating in "decline". History has seen this process repeated in various parts of the world.

Arnold Toynbee, on the other hand, did not believe that the developmental processes of civilization were of an identical pattern. Employing the ideas of "challenge and response" in *A Study of History*, Toynbee argued that even under similar natural conditions (challenges), civilizations responded differently, which gave rise to varied patterns of development.

Tehranian: The subject of "civilization" is eternally fascinating. You have already outlined the general views of Spengler and Toynbee, both of whom employed organic metaphors to suggest that civilizations, like organisms, pass through cycles of birth, youth, maturity, old age, and death.

There are also others, such as Karl Marx, Max Weber, Sigmund Freud, Pitirim A. Sorokin, Norbert Elias, and numerous anthropologists, who have concerned themselves with the problems of culture and civilization, how they emerge, develop, decline, and die.

Ikeda: I have had a deep personal interest in views of civilizational history, which led to a ten-day long dialogue on the subject at Dr. Toynbee's house in London. That was about thirty years ago, and I still have fond memories of our conversations.

In the record of our dialogue, *Choose Life* (Oxford University Press, London, 1976), Toynbee rejected the notion that the natural environment determines the level of creativity of a people, and instead emphasized the crucial importance of how people respond to environmental difficulties as the source of creativity.

Tehranian: I've read *Choose Life* with much interest.

The West-centered View of History and Cultural Hegemony

Ikeda: One of Toynbee's major contributions, I think, was his presentation of an antithesis to the once-dominant view of history centered on the West.

The progress of cultural anthropology and other factors have helped to destroy the preponderance of Western values, and cultural relativism that denies a hierarchical order among cultures has taken firm root by now. Toynbee was a pioneer in a way in spreading a more balanced view of history.

Tehranian: I think that is very correct. Up until then, the prevailing Western attitude had been that the West was at the pinnacle of what is considered to be "civilized" in comparison with other cultures and civilizations lagging behind.

Such a view has lost its credibility completely today. In any case, it was only in the last two centuries that the West could boast of its "advanced" civilization. No historians would seriously claim the superiority of the West in other eras.

Ikeda: Earlier in our discussion, we talked about how the Islamic world influenced Europe. Now there is a common recognition that the West has not always predominated.

Tehranian: A stark example of the West-centered view of history was seen in the rigid application of the evolutionary theory by the 19th-century anthropologist Edward Tylor. His 1895 statement reads in part, "Human life can be roughly classified into three great stages, Savage, Barbaric, Civilized … A savage of the Brazilian forests, a barbarous New Zealander or Dahoman, and a civilized European …".

This Western hubris was not seriously challenged until two Western-sponsored world wars, a cold war, several genocides, the nuclear threat, and an environmental crisis demonstrated its vacuity.

Ikeda: Having witnessed the storms of "inhumanity" and numerous tragedies that raged in Europe, for all the "refinement" and "advancement" of its civilization, one begins to wonder what is really barbarous and what is really progress.

Meanwhile, we shouldn't go to the other extreme, jumping to the conclusion that civilizations other than Western are superior. Such a biased view gets us nowhere. We should take utmost care not to fall into cultural hegemonism by considering one's own civilization absolute. The dangers of cultural hegemonism are inherent not just in Western but in any other civilization.

Tehranian: In recent years, scholars such as Edward Said, Michel Foucault, and Noam Chomsky have also shown how such hegemonic projects emerge not so much out of any inherent superiority of a culture over others but in pursuit of power and preeminence. In fact, in an age of globalization, we can no longer speak of cultural superiority or inferiority. Rather, we must focus on cultural dialogue and negotiation.

Ikeda: That is precisely what our own dialogue is aimed at.

Tehranian: True. We are entering a post-hegemonic era in which dialogue and negotiation of meaning will be more important than force and domination.

Civilization: A Way to Organize Cultures

Tehranian: Before we go further, let me clarify the conceptual differences between culture and civilization.

Ikeda: Yes, the two terms are often confused.

Tehranian: I consider "culture" as an expression of human life forms and "civilization" as attempts to control and direct the cultural forms into particular material and/or moral formations.

Civilizations are thus more consciously organized and more complex social systems, including legal, technological, economic, and political constructs encompassing a variety of cultures. There is, for instance, a Western civilization encompassing British, French, German, American and other cultures.

There is also a global human civilization emerging out of the contributions of various Eastern, Western, Southern, and Northern civilizations. In this sense, civilization is a useful category of analysis.

Ikeda: With growing globalization in recent decades, the term "a global civilization" is certainly taking on a realistic meaning. But the current trend toward globalization seems to lack direction, which in turn has given rise to new destabilizing factors.

Insofar as globalization is an irreversible trend, we need a solid vision or philosophy that provides a clear direction in which globalization should proceed.

Tehranian: Right. Since every civilization maximizes certain values and norms, sometimes at the expense of others, we also need to have some clarity on what constitutes a desirable norm for the global civilization that is in process of formation.

My proposal is to consider dialogue and the movement from cultural narcissism to cultural altruism as a basis for such a civilizational development. This begins with the premise that ethnocentrism is still a universal phenomenon. In other words, most cultural formations consider themselves superior to others unless and until they encounter Toynbeean challenges from inside or outside. That is how new and more effective values are created. The genius of Soka Gakkai is to recognize and value this process.

Ikeda: That's exactly the point. In my January 26, 1998 peace proposal, I introduced the idea of "humanitarian competition" first advocated by Tsunesaburo Makiguchi, by which he meant "benefiting oneself while benefiting others". Based on that idea, I called for changing our behavioral norm from "competition" to "collaborative value creation". I believe such a shift is necessary to open up a new path to "global civilization" based on "tolerance" and "symbiosis"—a third path that will lead neither to a uniform world order dominated by a certain set of values nor to a chaotic and mosaic world order.

Tehranian: I wholeheartedly agree with you. Humankind must undergo basic transformation in values to shift from cultural narcissism to cultural altruism.

Intercultural Contacts: Japan and the West

Tehranian: Let us now take a look at history at this point. Generally, the response to intercultural challenges ranges from *rejection* to *imitation* and *adaptation*. The encounter of most Asian cultures with the West can illustrate the point. The case of Japan especially demonstrates that the initial response of the Japanese to the West was total rejection of "the barbarians".

Ikeda: That is correct. The term "southern barbarians" was a symbolic one, in that it connoted not only contempt but a sense of awe and incompatibility *vis-à-vis* the unknown, I think.

This was in the mid-16th century (1549), toward the end of the Muromachi period, when St. Francis Xavier, the Jesuit missionary, landed in Japan. The term "southern barbarians" was used from the late Muromachi period into the Edo period.

Tehranian: Subsequently, Japan attempted to seal off its borders to Western penetration. Following Commodore Perry's arrival three centuries later in 1853, however, Japan could no longer resist Western power and cultural domination. In 1854, Japan signed a treaty of amity and commerce with the United States, opting for a course of action imitating the West in order to achieve preeminence in the world.

The Meiji Restoration made that option decisive, but the degree of imitation went further in the 20th century to include also the imitation of Western imperialism and militarism.

Ikeda: As you say, Dr. Tehranian, Japan indeed embarked on the road to build "a rich country, a strong army" in order to join the ranks of the Western powers. Lest it lag behind in the race for colonial domination, Japan in those days was involved in foreign wars almost constantly, invading its Asian neighbors over and over.

As a result, Japan ended up making enemies of almost all the countries of the world until it was defeated at the hands of the Allied Powers in World War II.

Tehranian: Their defeat in World War II taught the Japanese that they must go through reconstruction by abandoning militarism and bringing in the latest science and technology from the West.

Through cultural movements such as Soka Gakkai, some Japanese have also reached out to the rest of the world by promoting cultural exchange and dialogue to move away from cultural narcissism and toward cultural altruism. The SGI, the international version of Soka Gakkai, is committed to the spirit of dialogue and the Nichiren Buddhist values of universal nonviolence and compassion.

In any case, if my reading of Japanese cultural history is near the mark, I believe we can apply it to other countries, cultures, and civilizations, as well.

Ikeda: Your understanding of Japan's cultural history is very accurate. I also appreciate your kind words about our movement.

The basic orientation of Soka Gakkai was already firmly established before the war when it was founded. The first president Tsunesaburo Makiguchi advocated the idea of "humanitarian competition" as mentioned earlier in his *A Geography of Human Life* at the very beginning of this century (1903). Japan was moving headlong toward the goal of "a rich country, a strong army" at that very moment.

After the war, Soka Gakkai, continuing on Makiguchi's ideal, launched a vigorous movement for peace, culture, and education based on Buddhist philosophy.

Paragraph 8 of the SGI Charter, issued in the Fall of 1995, reads:

> SGI shall respect cultural diversity and promote cultural exchange, thereby creating an international society of mutual understanding and harmony.

Scientific-Technological Progress and Human Morality

Tehranian: Scientific and technological development, it may seem, has made it possible for humankind to enjoy unprecedented prosperity, hitherto unknown affluence. But as the example of the twentieth century has shown, there are no guarantees that moral or spiritual advance can match material progress. This century has been at once a century of stunning material progress and the bloodiest era in all recorded human history.

As kill/hit ratios have advanced with weapons of mass destruction, there has not developed a comparable moral or institutional restraint on the use of violence for settling international disputes. And, in war, human beings turn into true barbarians, discarding most codes of civilized behavior.

Ikeda: As you have just pointed out, the 20th century has had both extremely bright and seamy sides. Stanford University professor emeritus Kenneth J. Arrow believes that this has been the best century insofar as longevity, economic growth, democratic institutions, and individual freedom are concerned, but that it has also been the worst century in the sense that it has resulted in an astronomical number of victims of war, large and small, and politically motivated massacres, while destruction of the global environment has accelerated.

Professor Arrow describes the two-facedness of the century as a direct reflection of human duality—the tendency toward evil and the proclivity toward goodness and moderation. I, too, feel strongly that as far as human morality goes, we still have a long way to go—so many problems lie ahead of us.

Tehranian: I agree with you. An especially important question here is the relation between moral and technological advance. Can we really consider a nation that is more technologically advanced as more "civilized" than the ones that are not? Clearly not, particularly if we consider the criterion that I have proposed earlier, i.e. the movement from cultural narcissism to cultural altruism.

Altruism requires a system of values and a state of mind that enables us to empathize with the suffering of others. Altruistic cultures cannot turn others into objects for us to manipulate or destroy.

Ikeda: Empathy with the suffering of others—that's really one of the key qualities necessary in making coexistence with others a reality.

French philosopher Simone Weil (1909–43) had this to say: "Pride about the greatness of a nation is essentially exclusionary, hence cannot be shared by other nations. By contrast, concern about the plight of others is essentially universal." Basing her thinking on this idea of shared concern, Weil sought the possibility of a more universal humanism. In "altruistic sympathy" she found the key to overcoming the narrow-minded pride about one's group—the "we" consciousness.

Tehranian: I can cite any number of terms that express such narrow-minded pride, what I call cultural narcissism. "The White Man's burden", "Manifest Destiny", "Deutschland über alles", and "Japan, the Land of [Shinto] Gods" are but a few examples.

Such slogans as "above all nations is humanity" and "think globally and act locally" and expressions like "Spaceship Earth" and "The Gaia Hypothesis" are examples of the burgeoning of a global civilization.

Ikeda: Buddhism, too, teaches the importance of "empathy for the suffering of others" as the source of human solidarity across cultures and races. "Compassion" that arises from such "empathy" is the very core of the spirit of Buddhism.

Tehranian: I understand that perfectly well. Restoring humanity in terms of "empathy for the suffering of others" is the most urgent task of our time. To that end, we must establish altruism, not egotism, as a new value governing relations among people. In our relations with other people and nature, we should not judge others simply on the basis of our narrow self-interest or treat them as objects of manipulation to realize our own selfish ends.

I feel, nevertheless, that we still have a long way to go before we can reach Martin Buber's vision of an "I-Thou" rather than "I-It" relationship with the rest of humanity and nature, treating others as having value unto themselves.

Ikeda: Yes, but we should never give up. No matter how slow and inconspicuous, we must move on steadily, step by step.

Tehranian: You're absolutely right. Unless we do, there will be no hope for the future of humankind.

Implications of the "Clash of Civilizations" Thesis

Ikeda: Whether or not clash or conflict between civilizations is unavoidable—this question has become a major focus of attention in the debates on post-Cold War international politics. The current debate was in a way triggered by Harvard University professor Samuel Huntington's "Clash of Civilizations" article published in the Summer, 1993 issue of *Foreign Affairs*.

Tehranian: That's right. His sensational thesis initiated a heated debate for and against.

Ikeda: Professor Huntington classifies the post-Cold War world, marked by the end of ideological confrontation, into eight civilizations—Chinese, Japanese, Hindu, Islamic, Western, Russian Orthodox, Latin American, and African. He then predicts that the clash of civilizations will shape world politics in the next century, and that the differences between civilizations will draw the dividing lines of future international disputes. He cites as evidence the outbreak of many conflicts in areas along the boundaries of civilizations, including the former Yugoslavia, Central Asia, and the Middle East.

Tehranian: His thesis pitting the "West against the Rest" (of civilizations) echoes some 19th-century notions. I'd like to point out its contributions, however, before going on with some criticisms.

The thesis has helped in problematizing culture, civilization, values, morality, and norms in international relations. It has also contributed to the weakening of the state-centric views of foreign affairs.

Ikeda: Could you elaborate on that?

Tehranian: Well, Huntington belongs to a generation of American political scientists who identified themselves as realists, generally arguing that values and morality should have no or little place in the conduct of international relations. They argued that whereas domestic life is based upon moral consensus, international life is devoid of such a consensus.

In the words of the founder of the realist school Hans Morgenthau (1904–80), the conduct of foreign policy should follow one and only one guiding star, that is, the national interest. It was belief in such theories that led the United States into the tragedy of the wars in Korea, Vietnam, and the Persian Gulf.

Ikeda: When you consider the national interest as supreme and defy morality in international society, then war becomes simply one of the options in the conduct of foreign relations. A country guided by such a way of thinking is easily tempted to go to war—that is precisely the pitfall of giving top priority to the national interest. Are you implying that Professor Huntington is not one of those so-called realists?

Tehranian: Yes. In that sense, Professor Huntington may be considered a revisionist. As a neo-realist, he has now acknowledged the central importance of cultures, civilizations, norms, and values in international relations. However, this recognition has taken a traditional geopolitical and realist turn.

Under-emphasizing the great cultural diversities of the world, he has identified certain territories with certain civilizations and argued that the West is a distinctly different civilization from the Rest. There are also subtle and sometimes not so subtle hints in his analysis that somehow the West is superior and therefore more justified in pursuing its "civilizing" mission in the rest of the world. In particular, according to Professor Huntington, a Chinese-Islamic alliance presents a particular threat to Western values and views and must be therefore confronted.

Three-point Criticism of the Huntington Thesis

Ikeda: True, the post-Cold War world has seen local conflicts break out one after another as if the latent contradictions had surfaced all at once. There have also been serious economic confrontations accompanying the worldwide recession. Undeniably, the world situation continues to be volatile.

It was perhaps against this backdrop that the Huntington article had such a strong impact on the thinking of many people, whether they agreed with him or not. I, for one, have some serious doubts about analyzing such an intricate problem simply in terms of the "clash of civilizations". There is a danger that his thesis may mislead people to assume that conflicts are inevitable insofar as civilizations vary.

Future prospects often affect our present behavior. That is why we must carefully examine such theses as Professor Huntington's.

Tehranian: I agree with you completely. As I see it, the Huntington thesis is cultural narcissism in a new guise. It can be criticized on three distinctly different grounds—philosophical, empirical, and practical.

Philosophically, cultural narcissism of any kind gives rise to cultural narrow-mindedness and discrimination. Such narrow-mindedness is contrary to the needs of our own age of globalization requiring intercultural dialogue.

It may be argued that certain values demand universal application, especially those of human rights as enshrined in the Universal Declaration of Human Rights and its ancillary documents. It is simplistic to equate civilizations with geographic territories and to essentialize their values as if there are no tensions within each civilization.

Ikeda: I suppose so, but the idea of the human rights that humanity should share must be something more than an external norm. It must have the kind of universality that is generated from within. I mean the concepts of equality and human dignity that are formulated through a fundamental examination of a person's internal life.

During the 1993 World Conference on Human Rights held in Vienna, the industrialized countries and developing nations were divided sharply over the definition of human rights. The universality of human rights was a focus of debate at the meeting, but that idea should be thoroughly examined in terms of what I have just said.

Otherwise, we will never be able to break through the stalemate in the arguments.

Tehranian: I think I know what you mean. As a review of history shows, ever since the introduction of the Lotus Sutra, Hammurabi's Code, the Ten Commandments, the Magna Carta, the US Declaration of Independence, and the Universal Declaration, the discourse on human rights has been part of the world cultural negotiation and consensus formation. No single country or civilization can claim monopoly ownership.

Ikeda: Very true, indeed. Instead of claiming monopoly on the human rights concept simply to demonstrate the foresightedness and superiority of their cultures, the countries of the world ought to concentrate on open dialogue and sincere cooperation on ways to realize human rights through all corners of the globe.

Tehranian: I think so, too. Empirically, also, Professor Huntington's analysis is seriously flawed. Although national cultures and regional civilizations are still useful categories of analysis, the processes of rapid globalization through the global marketplace, migration, and communications are creating prevalent conditions of cultural hybridity.

Professor Huntington, however, is trying to resurrect the nineteenth century purist notions of nationalism under the guise of civilizational purity. Such purity exists only in the minds of the beholders.

Ikeda: In Japan, too, we find a deep-rooted notion, not at all based in the facts of history, that the Japanese are a homogeneous race. This kind of bias is fast becoming a mere fiction in the midst of rapid globalization.

Tehranian: Right. Today, with a few exceptions, no society can claim any purity of ethnicity or culture. Nearly all societies are multicultural and becoming more so under the impact of globalization.

It would be empirically more accurate to speak of how traditional cultures and civilizations are renewing themselves through intercultural dialogue, negotiation, borrowings, and adaptation rather than to focus on civilizational purity. The boundaries Professor Huntington has drawn around eight civilizations are blurred and arbitrary.

Ikeda: That's my feeling, too. His classification looks like it is more for classification's sake than anything else. The eight categories of civilization he presented seem to be conceptually too ambiguous and deficient in validity, according to many scholars.

The Complexity of Local Conflicts

Tehranian: Finally, practically speaking, the events of the post-Cold War era demonstrate how ill-suited Professor Huntington's thesis is for understanding international conflict and cooperation.

No grand generalization about civilizations can explain the rise of ethnonationalism as a force in the fragmentation processes of the post-Cold War era. None of the conflicts in Bosnia, the Caucasus, Persian Gulf, Israel-Palestine, Korea, and Africa can be adequately understood if we view them as civilizational conflicts.

Ikeda: I am also apprehensive about the easygoing schematization and simplification of such regional conflicts. If we tried to explain everything in terms of civilizational differences, we would not only lose sight of the true causes of conflict but end up instilling fixed ideas and misconceptions in people's minds. The "poisonous effects" of such stereotyped images can be more harmful and enduring than we imagine.

Tehranian: Exactly. The conflict in Bosnia, for example, is among three ethnic-political factions, including the Roman Catholic Croatians, the Orthodox Christian Serbs, and the Muslim Bosnians. However, ethnically and culturally, all three groups are Slavs. The conflict is among ethnic cousins who have been historically divided by reason of imperialist rivalries in the Balkans among the Ottoman, Austro-Hungarian, German, and Italian empires.

Ikeda: One scholar (German poet and critic, H. M. Entzenberger) described our time as a period of transition "from the Cold War to civil wars". The conflict in Bosnia in that sense is more like a civil war.

Tehranian: Yes. The conflict in the Caucasus is between Azerbaijan and Armenia, Georgia and Abkhazia, and Russia and Chechnya. In all three cases, the conflicts have little do to with civilizational conflicts and much to do with the rise of ethnic nationalism and conflicting territorial claims.

Islamic Iran and capitalist Russia side with Christian Armenia, while secular US and Turkey side with Azerbaijan. The main bone of contention is the Caspian Sea's oil resources and *not* civilizational claims.

Ikeda: I see. International conflicts in recent decades often involve, directly or indirectly, economic interests. I don't think we can ever talk about these conflicts without regard to the economic aspect. Oil resources, especially, are one of the decisive factors in international affairs. The advantages of the oil-producing countries are still undeniable.

Tehranian: In the Persian Gulf, the conflict is between the competing nationalisms of Iran, Iraq, Kuwait, Turkey, and Kurdistan, and between international oil interests and nationalist aspirations of the region. Thus, in the Persian Gulf War, we witnessed a cross-civilizational alliance of the Christian West with the fundamentalist Islamic Saudi Arabia and Kuwait against Saddam Hussein.

The Western media have often interpreted the Arab-Israel conflict as a religious or cultural conflict, but that is far from the truth. A close reading of history will show that the conflict is between two competing nationalisms claiming the same land on the basis of dubious religious justifications.

In Korea, the conflict is a relic of the Cold War era between two socio-economic systems in an ethnically homogeneous Korea, South and North.

In Africa, the conflict between various tribes has a lot to do with continuing African tribalism manipulated during the Cold War by the two superpowers to advance their own ends.

Ikeda: For all these reasons, you are saying that it is not realistic to apply Professor Huntington's thesis to various regional conflicts around the world. They all have their specific historical, political, economic, and cultural factors at play. You cannot and should not generalize about that which is the main factor and those factors that are secondary.

Tehranian: Exactly. After all this, though, there remains the question of why Professor Huntington's thesis has received such widespread attention around the world.

Ikeda: It seems to me that the degree of international attention his article received, rather than its content, bespeaks of the seriousness of the whole problem of civilization.

Tehranian: Right. I think there are two basic reasons. First, old prejudices die-hard. Political regimes in countries such as the United States, Russia, Iran, and Iraq, which are characterized by ethnic diversity, often need external enemies to build up national unity. In the absence of visible enemies, they tend to invent them.

Professor Huntington has provided a convenient grand theory for constructing enemies in both the East and the West. His views have a following among extremists in the United States as well as China and the Islamic world.

Ikeda: Professor Huntington's theory is being used as a convenient tool for agitating antagonisms by exclusionary, aggressive people in various countries. That's where I see the tragedy of it all.

I recall your writing about the Huntington thesis in an article published in *Seikyo Shimbun* (June 22, 1994). In it, you wrote, "Prof. Huntington's approach to the problem simply revived what was a menace in the past." "If you want an enemy to hate, it is possible to fabricate one in any way." "But inventing an enemy in this manner risks the danger of dividing a multiethnic, multi-religious society like that of the United States by a framework of loyalty to 'conflicting civilizations'."

Tehranian: Yes, I remember that. The other reason for the extraordinary attention given to the Huntington thesis is that since it has received a favorable reception in some foreign policy circles in the United States, the rest of the world has been curious about the strategic thinking of American foreign policy makers.

I must add that, fortunately, there are many voices of sanity in the United States warning against the implications of Professor Huntington's thesis for a belligerent foreign policy toward China and the Islamic world.

Ikeda: Thank you for your lucid explanations. We have no choice but to patiently promote "intercivilizational dialogues" in order to avoid the "clash of civilizations". It is no overstatement to say that the destiny of humankind in the 21st century rests on such an effort.

CHAPTER 7

Dialogue of Civilizations

Tehranian: On February 11, 1996 the Toda Institute for Global Peace and Policy Research was established and I was appointed its director. We now have the support and cooperation of a great many scholars around the world.

Ikeda: I hear that the *Honolulu Weekly* gave wide coverage to the Institute's activities.

Tehranian: They ran a three-page feature with the headline, "Planet Peace—The Toda Institute plays a part in moving the world's peoples toward common ground." It was a happy surprise.

This is just one example, but I see in recent years that there are a great many people who aspire for peace moving in more or less the same direction. I feel that a growing current for world peace is forming.

Ikeda: That does seem to be true. As we have already discussed, the UN General Assembly designated 2001 as "The Year of Dialogue Among Civilizations", and it has also decided to observe the "International Decade for a Culture of Peace and Non-Violence for the Children of the World" between 2001 and 2010.

The international community seems desperately anxious to abandon the repetition of violence and carnage that plagued this century and create a new "culture of peace and non-violence" in the next.

Tehranian: The future prospects for humanity diverge greatly depending on what sort of values guide the 21st century.

Ikeda: Absolutely. I hope our dialogue will help to provide a positive orientation for civilization in this new century.

Tehranian: As I see it, civilization is a system of more or less coherent ontology, epistemology, and praxiology. Ontologies provide us with an understanding of the origins and end of being, while epistemologies give us theories of knowledge and learning, and praxiologies supply codes of conduct. These three components come together in an organic relationship in any given civilization.

In this sense, there are bound to be differences among civilizations, but I reject all hierarchical notions of cultures and civilizations, of superiority and inferiority. Some civilizations are clearly more advanced technologically, but that does not spell out moral superiority.

Ikeda: I see your point very well. There may be differences between civilizations, but that in no way means that one is superior or inferior to another. That understanding is the basic premise of inter-civilizational dialogue.

Tehranian: You can, of course, provide typologies of material and moral progress along certain preconceived indices. But in my mind, all cultures and civilizations are products of human imagination devised to adapt to, transform, and transcend the universal human conditions of finitude, fragility, and moral frailty. Each culture and civilization in its own unique way offers its members ways of self-transcendence, moral fortitude, and resistance to force.

Ikeda: I agree that human imagination and dynamism for change, which is the product of human imagination, are what give life to cultures and civilizations.

Tehranian: Each culture and civilization is responding to the same mysteries of life in the context of its own unique ecological and historical situation. That is why, I believe, the differences are to be valued and celebrated as signs of human genius.

To speak of higher and lower civilizations is to miss the central value of diversity in the unfolding of human history. It is also a sign of cultural narcissism.

Neither Clash nor Coexistence

Ikeda: It seems to me that the differences between civilizations are not really what cause them to clash against each other. Rather, I wonder if it is not the prejudicial attitude of superiority that causes conflict between them.

We must rethink the either-or pattern of thinking itself—either "clash" or "coexistence" of civilizations. Even if "coexistence" were realized, it would not benefit humankind insofar as civilizations simply remained existing side by side.

Tehranian: Human thought is often trapped in dichotomies; that is, in antitheses such as light versus darkness, good versus evil, white versus black. That is the simplest and least sophisticated way of understanding the world.

Life is far more complex than that. There are gradations of light and darkness, of good and evil, and of white and black. To understand these subtleties, we need to expand the parameters of our discourse. In Chinese philosophy, the concepts of yin and yang suggest a way out of the tyranny of dichotomies. We are invited to think no longer in either/or terms but in categories of both/and. Yin and yang suggest the universal interdependence of light and darkness, good and evil, life and death. The problem is no longer to make a clear-cut choice but to maintain a balance.

Ikeda: Besides the concepts of yin and yang, Eastern philosophy has many worldviews that are quite different from Western dualism. In Buddhism, for instance, we have the idea that good and evil are one and the same. This teaching points not just to the interdependence between good and evil but to the way to transcend the two.

An encounter between civilizations is not evil in itself. The problem is what the result will be. Philosopher Karl Popper (1902–94) argued that the risk arising from inter-civilizational contact is undoubtedly large, but that such contact can also be a major source of cultural creativity.

Examples abound in history where contacts between different civilizations led to the blossoming of rich cultures and the creation of new values—the meeting of Chinese and Indian civilizations via the Silk Road and the mingling of Greek and Islamic civilizations in the Mediterranean area, to name only two.

Tehranian: Very true. Tensions among civilizations can, indeed, be creative or destructive or probably both.

Ikeda: Whether or not the energies generated by cross-cultural contacts can be channeled into something really creative depends, I think, on efforts on both sides, that is, "dialogue".

To cite Karl Popper again, when two or more cultures come into contact, people are made to realize that the way of life and customs they have taken for granted for a long time are neither something ordained by God nor an essential part of human nature. Popper says history is precisely the process of coming to this realization.

Put another way, human history progressed as people discovered that their culture is not something natural or unique. Differences can provide positive stimuli for people in their objective appraisal of their cultural roots in comparison with other, alien civilizations. The accumulation of such encounters can open up new prospects.

Tehranian: That's exactly the goal of inter-civilizational dialogue.

In Platonic dialogue, truth is considered as the search for truth via reasoned conversation, clashes, and convergence of views. In Hegelian and Marxian dialectics, progress consists of unity of opposites in order to arrive at a synthesis of thesis and antithesis.

Ikeda: Friends and foes—such a simple, dualistic schematization is not only inaccurate but very dangerous because it is likely to breed prejudices in people's minds.

In this age of information, images tend to precede everything else, often distorted and diffused, which blocks truth. All this makes it all the more important for people to talk to each other face-to-face.

Tehranian: In this connection, let me introduce an interesting book entitled *Hyperspace* by the noted theoretical physicist Michio Kaku. He identifies ten dimensions of reality. We are fully aware of only the four dimensions of space (length, width, and depth) and time. String theory in physics has mathematically demonstrated the next six dimensions.

We are so trapped in our four dimensions that we experience the other dimensions as fleeting moments. It is therefore wise to be modest about our claims to knowledge.

Ikeda: Exactly. Inter-civilizational dialogue based on open-mindedness and modesty will be the key to overcoming antagonism and elevating relations among people to a higher plane. What I advocate is neither clash nor side-by-side existence, but a third way—shared prosperity through "inter-civilizational dialogue".

The Spirit of Dialogue in the "Questions of King Milinda"

Ikeda: Let us now review several cases from history. "Inter-civilizational dialogue" reminds me first of the well-known Buddhist sutra *Milindapanha* [The Questions of King Milinda]. It is a record of the dialogues of the Buddhist monk Nagasena and the Greco-Bactrian King Milinda, who ruled northwestern India about 2,100 years ago in the latter half of the 2nd century B.C.

It was a time following Alexander the Great's expedition, when Greek and Indian civilizations came into contact, stimulating each other.

Tehranian: The dialogue is famous as the occasion of the great spiritual encounter of Western reason and Eastern wisdom.

Ikeda: Especially noteworthy was the fact that both stuck with the "logic of the scholar" throughout, never resorting to the "logic of the king".

Before they begin their dialogue, Nagasena says to the king: "Your Majesty, if you will discourse with the logic of the scholar, I will carry on the conversation with you. If, on the other hand, Your Majesty wants to discuss with the logic of the king, I will not engage in any dialogue with you."

At that point, King Milinda asks the monk to explain the differences between the logic of the scholar and the logic of the king.

Nagasena replies as follow:

> When scholars talk a matter over with one another, then there is winding up, an unravelling; one or the other is convicted of error, and he then acknowledges his mistake; distinctions are drawn, and contra-distinctions; and yet, thereby, they are not angered. Thus do scholars, O King, discuss.
>
> When a king, your Majesty, discusses a matter, and he advances a point, if any one differ from him on that point, he is apt to fine him, saying: 'Inflict such and such punishment upon that fellow!' Thus, your Majesty, do kings discuss. (T. W. Rhys Davids and Hermann Oldenberg, 1965)

King Milinda understood the profound meaning of Nagasena's words, and a long and very fruitful series of dialogues thus began between the two.

Tehranian: The perspective provided by this episode is relevant in our own time. The Milindapanha sutra has parallels in other cultural traditions as well. Force and dialogue are two ends of the same spectrum in any communication.

The logic of the king is force; the logic of the scholar is dialogue. You can achieve power through a bayonet but you cannot sit on a bayonet. Even kings have to use the power of dialogue if they hope to extend their rule. This point has been driven home by political philosophers as diverse as Plato, Aristotle, Nizam al-Mulk, Farabi, Ibn-Rushd (Averroes) Machiavelli, Hobbes, Locke, and Rousseau.

Ikeda: Regrettable as it is, dialogue has yet to take a dominant place in the world. I believe that "the logic of the scholar", Nagasena's symbolic term, shows why we need to carry on rational, open dialogue in any age. Buddhists, ever since Shakyamuni, have abided by this logic to conduct dialogue on a free, equal basis.

It is amazing to realize that more than 2,000 years ago the Greek and Indian men of wisdom gave us such a valuable model.

Habermas's Theory of Communication

Tehranian: In considering the modern significance of "the Questions of King Milinda", I think it will be useful to look at the concept of "communicative rationality" advanced by German philosopher and sociologist Jürgen Habermas. He has focused on "communicative rationality" as a basis for democratic development. He makes a distinction between this and other types of rationality, including practical, instrumental, and critical.

Practical rationality is what we often call "common sense" in any specific cultural tradition. However, what is common sense in one culture may prove to be common nonsense in another. In the Western world, for instance, tipping for services extended to you at a restaurant or hotel is common practice, but not in Japan.

In the capitalist West, service is a commodity like any other for which you have to pay 10, 15, or 20 percent. In Japan, service is considered an honor, the value of which is actually diminished by the attempt to tip. Both customs make sense within their particular cultural contexts.

Ikeda: Habermas is saying, in other words, that practical rationality is valid only within a specific community or human group.

Tehranian: Correct. Instrumental rationality is comparatively more universal. It is based on the rational calculations of how to accomplish a task or achieve an objective in the most cost-effective way. Science and technology are the methods of instrumental rationality in which the entire world, including society and individuals, are considered as objects of manipulation to achieve certain goals.

Unlike these two types of rationality, critical rationality begins with certain normative ideals with which we compare, contrast, and criticize existing conditions. All moral and ideological schools thus participate in the exercise of this kind of rationality by criticizing their worlds from the perspective of their ideal world.

Ikeda: There are many examples in our time of people or groups of people who regard their own theoretical constructs or models as absolute and keep criticizing existing realities that do not conform to their ideals. The 20th century has witnessed numerous tragedies caused by the spell of ideology, a situation reminiscent of Procrustes's bed.

Procrustes was the legendary robber of ancient Greece who forced his victims to fit into a certain bed by stretching or lopping off their legs. Similarly, man-made theories and ideologies have become dangerous weapons that force individuals into conformity with or subservient to a system or doctrine, pushing both people and society into a state of desolation and putting a stranglehold on their lives.

Tehranian: Habermas's communicative rationality, by contrast, does not begin with ideal constructs except for one that he calls "ideal speech community", characterized by the absence of force and the presence of equality in communicative access and competence of all participants in dialogue.

Obviously, such conditions do not exist in the real world. But we can approximate them by creating the conditions of freedom and equality in communication. Despite the barriers of time, space, and culture, our own dialogue is a clear example of such communicative rationality in line with the "logic of the scholar".

Ikeda: Habermas writes that a sincere speaker is obligated, by the tacit premise that he speaks with seriousness, to be responsible for the consequences of his verbal commitment.

As you have pointed out, sincerity and open-mindedness on both sides are indispensable for genuine dialogue. In that sense, Habermas' thesis for "discourses without dominance", merits a positive evaluation. He took exception to the thinking that treats communication exclusively as a tool of strategy.

Rùmi's Universal Outlook

Ikeda: Besides the logic of the scholar, I believe another essential condition for fruitful dialogue is a universalistic outlook that enables people to transcend differences in cultural background and environment.

So, let us next focus on Jalal-ud-din Rùmi (1207–73), arguably one of the three greatest of Persian poets, along with Mosleh al-Din Sa'adi (ca. 1184–1291) and Hafez (ca. 1326–90).

Rùmi was a "poet of inter-civilizational dialogue" who lived in Persia in the same period that Nichiren Daishonin (1222–82) was active in Japan. It was the time of the Mongol Empire's territorial expansion throughout much of Eurasia.

Tehranian: Yes. The 13th century was a time of great turmoil in West and Central Asia. The Mongol invasion had devastated vast areas of the ancient world and put an end, in 1258, to the Abbasid Caliphate in Baghdad.

Cities with over one million people such as Neishapur had been completely ruined, with no living creatures left in them. According to historians, even cats and dogs were not spared. Under such calamitous circumstances, life was precarious and despair clawed at people's spirits.

Ikeda: During such a period of upheaval, Rùmi was born in the city of Balkh (Ancient Bactria) in the northern part of what is today Afghanistan.

Tehranian: That's right. Rùmi came from a family of distinguished Muslim jurists. His father was the *sultan al-ulema* (king of the learned) in the city of Balkh. One of Rùmi's poems goes as follows:

There are many Turks who cannot truly speak to one another.
There are many Turks and Indians who intimately speak to each other.
The language of the heart is thus different from the language of the tongue.

Ikeda: Together with his parents, Rùmi moved from Persia to Iraq, then to Arabia and Syria, until they settled in a city called Konya in Asia Minor (present-day Turkey). I have the feeling that the spirit nurtured through those years of travel in his youth is encapsulated in the words you have just quoted.

Tehranian: Your focus on Rùmi as a poet of inter-civilizational dialogue is extremely apt. The words that you cited are ample proof.

Rùmi served as a bridge between two civilizations by bringing together the teachings of the Buddha and Islam—two cultural heritages born in different regions.

At this point, let me explain a little about the regional characteristics of Central Asia where Rùmi was born and grew up.

Central Asia as a Crossroads of Civilizations

Tehranian: From 600 B.C. to 600 A.D., Bactria was the center of an Iranian, Greek, and Indian civilization. As a satrapy of the Persian Empire, Balkh, Rùmi's birthplace, fell to Alexander the Great in 328 B.C. It declared its independence in 250 B.C. and became a powerful state, known to the Greeks as Bactria, carrying conquests deep into Northern India. That brought it into contact with Hinduism and Buddhism.

The rise of the Kushana Dynasty in Central Asia subsequently provided a politically favorable environment for the growth of Buddhism. Buddhism was introduced into China by missionaries from Central Asia, and later from India about the time of Christ.

Ikeda: The Soka University Silk Road Expedition, as part of its scholarly exchange program with Uzbekistan, carried out joint excavations of important archaeological sites along the Silk Road in 1989, 1991, and 1993.

There are many sites from the Kushana Dynasty period—remains of fortresses and settlements. The Dalvarzintepa site that the Soka University team excavated is said to have been a major fortress of the Kushana Dynasty.

Mahayana Buddhism flourished in India at the time of the Kushana Dynasty, which reached its peak in the 1st–3rd centuries. Gandhara culture, too, flourished under the same dynasty. King Kanishka, known as the most outstanding monarch of the Kushana Dynasty, was a great patron of Buddhism. The Fourth Buddhist Council was held under his patronage. Famous Mahayana scholars like Nagarjuna and Ashvagosha were active in his day.

Tehranian: I have had the privilege of reading *Antiquities of Southern Uzbekistan* that documents Soka University's findings. To understand how Central Asia became a crossroads of trade and cultural traffic, including the spread of Buddhism, we must know this sort of historical background.

Through the Silk Road, merchants from East and West exchanged their goods, while the learned passed on their wisdom across the boundaries of religious and political traditions.

Ikeda: The influence of Gandhara on Chinese Buddhist art is evident from the groups of statues in the "Caves of the Thousand Buddhas" and the wall paintings at Dunhuang.

According to some experts, had it not been for the rise of Buddhism under King Kanishka's patronage, its development as a world religion might have been slowed down for a long time. The King's role in Buddhist history cannot be overemphasized.

Tehranian: When I was visiting Afghanistan in 1971 and Central Asia in 1992 and 1994, I became witness to the glories of this multi-cultural heritage.

Ikeda: Yes, I remember your telling me that you were on your way to the Silk Road when we first met in Tokyo in July 1992.

Tehranian: During my 1971 trip, on the banks of Amu Darya on the border of Afghanistan and the former Soviet Union, I witnessed the ruins of a Greek city-state preserved very much intact. On the vast Bamiyan plain, a few miles outside of Kabul, I witnessed the magnificent statues of Buddha carved into the surrounding mountains with the tallest reaching 53 meters high.

The temples of the monks were situated behind the statues. The Bamiyan plain itself had served as a gathering place for thousands of Buddhist pilgrims coming from all over Asia to worship together.

In the Kabul museum, I ran into a totally unique art form combining Greek and Buddhist features and symbols into its design of statues and ornaments. Unfortunately the museum has been destroyed by the civil war in Afghanistan. Despite international protest in 2002, the Taliban destroyed the statues of Buddha and the fresco paintings inside the caves.

Restoration of Humanity—Which Light? From Which Lamp?

Ikeda: Central Asia has also developed close relations with Islam, hasn't it?

Tehranian: Yes, it has. When Islam reached Central Asia in the 7th century, it had no choice but to enter into a dialogue with all the past cultural traditions of the region. They included Hinduism, Buddhism, Taoism, Hellenism, and Iranianism (Zoroastrianism, Mithraism, Manicheanism, and Mazdakism). Islam thus brought the religious and cultural contributions of the Semites (Jews, Christians, and Muslims) into an already rich cultural gold mine.

Ikeda: Am I correct in understanding that Sufism (Islamic mysticism) emerged out of the confluence of many cultures and civilizations?

Tehranian: Yes, it did. Although Sufism used Islamic metaphors and symbols, its content was thoroughly ecumenical and multicultural. Its synthesizing role was focused on the spirit rather than the letter of the law, the Way (*Tariqa*) rather than the Law (*Shari'a*), the reasons of the heart rather than the reasons of the mind, the inner truth rather than the outer forms and rituals, the worship of essences rather than idols, the Unity of Being rather than variations in life.

The message of Sufism is close to that of Taoism. Like Taoism, it points to the Way and provides poetry as the vehicle.

Ikeda: In one of his poems, Rùmi writes:

> Alight in the same place are ten lamps.
> They all vary in shape,
> But gazing at their collective light
> You cannot tell which light
> Comes from which of the lamps.
>
> In the realm of the spirit
> You find no partition whatsoever,
> No individuation whatsoever.

As Rùmi, who went so far as to envision the unity of humankind, tells us, even if there were hundreds of countries and thousands of ethnic groups, there must be the universal light of "humanity" burning in the innermost depths of diversity. What is important now is to burn the light of humanity in the heart of each and every person and bring all those lights together. That, I believe, is also the best way to give life to diverse ethnic and cultural traditions.

The Magnificent Cosmos—A Sense of Symbiotic Order

Tehranian: Our own times are not dissimilar to those of the 13th century West and Central Asia. Despite the great scientific and technological progress we have made, the anxieties of constant change and ceaseless desire in our acquisitive societies have combined with the anonymity and abstraction of life in a bureaucratic world to render the individual spiritually homeless.

Ikeda: Czech president Vaclav Havel described the human condition of our time as a crisis in "our ability to be our own masters".

Tehranian: We live sometimes in a meaningless world without belief, community, or direction. The search for meaning in such a world has led thoughtful and sensitive people to look beyond their own limited cultural horizons into other cultures and civilizations for answers to their perplexities.

That, in my mind, explains the growth of Soka Gakkai International (SGI) in many parts of the world, of Islam in Africa and the United States, and of Christianity in the former Soviet Union and China. Wherever you go, you can witness the search for ecumenical meanings that transcend xenophobic nationalism, ethnocentrism, and cultural narcissism.

Ikeda: I discussed the problem of what you have called "ecumenical meanings" in my lecture at the Moscow State University in 1994 under the title, "The Magnificent Cosmos".

The Lotus Sutra, using a simile, teaches how every person can find the same jewel (i.e. Buddha nature). If all people, belonging to different cultures and civilizations, should attain a cosmic self-awareness through their discovery of the inherent Buddha nature, then we would find humanity, nature, and the universe coexisting in harmony, with the micro-cosmos and the macro-cosmos fusing into a single entity of life. The kind of universality that emerges there might be called the sense of symbiotic order. And if people of the world should infuse their lives with such a sense of universality, then dialogue and mutual understanding among different ethnic and cultural groups would be possible. This was the gist of my speech.

Tehranian: That's a profoundly philosophic statement. Commensurate with this yearning for ecumenical meanings, new myths are emerging today to replace the old myths of Chosen People, Manifest Destiny, or White Man's Burden.

The Gaia Hypothesis, which considers the earth to be a living organism, is such a powerful universal myth that it may bring nations and tribes together in common efforts to protect and enhance Mother Earth. Founding myths such as this one form the ultimate basis of any civilization. Belief in the superiority of a particular race or nation often leads to the rise of imperialism, war, and destruction.

Ikeda: Underlying the various ethnic conflicts erupting today in many parts of the world, I believe, is the insularity of extreme ethnic consciousness.

In the same Moscow State University speech mentioned earlier, I quoted from Leo Tolstoy's *Anna Karenina*. The protagonist Levin throws cold water on the self-destructive ethnic passion that made the Serbo-Turkish war seem heroic by saying, "Yet it's not a question of sacrificing themselves only, but of killing the Turks".

Tehranian: The insanity of war blinds people to such an obvious fact.

Ikeda: Lurking in such insanity is the evil that drives people to commit inhumane atrocities against other groups without a second thought.

Levin ponders the manifestation of the divine that he feels within himself. He perceives it as supreme happiness and asks:

> Is that happiness restricted to Christians? What about the followers of other religions such as 'the Jews, the Mohammedans, the Confucians, the Buddhists' ...?

It was undoubtedly an inner revelation that Levin felt within himself. Then he poses questions about the Christians and pagans. Doubts of this sort are an expression of an inner power that propels introspection and self-renewal in the context of universality.

Tehranian: That's precisely the key for overcoming religious dogmatism. As we all well know, religious dogma has engendered countless tragedies throughout human history.

Ikeda: This inner power is the source of the humility and generosity of the spirit that have been at the core of ethical human values since ancient times and that are the basic ingredients of meaningful dialogue.

When religion ignores the importance of inner power and self-reflection, it risks becoming tyrannical and arrogant, and all too often becomes the rationale for human beings to harm and even kill one another "for the sake of religion". This sort of perversion has taken place over and over again in religious history.

We must stand on the common ground of "humanity", not "for the sake of religion". The SGI movement for "human revolution" is aimed solely at the inner transformation of individuals, who together will seek to rectify the perversion of history and create a bright, new global civilization.

Tehranian: The time has come for us to embrace an axial principle such as the Gaia Hypothesis, itself based on much scientific evidence, in order to unify the world against war, ignorance, and injustice.

A global civilization must be founded, as you have noted, on a "human revolution" that considers the Spaceship Earth as a vehicle for our common journey of discovery toward inter-civilizational peace, friendship, and transcendence.

CHAPTER 8

In Search of Global Ethics

Freedom from Greed, Dogma, and Illusion

Tehranian: Your earlier explanation of why Shakyamuni abandoned the secular world was very enlightening. He had discovered that the causes of human suffering are not just "tragic situations" like poverty and sickness, but more fundamental troubles rooted in the human heart—egoistic preoccupation with self-other distinctions, as between the healthy and sick or between young and old.

I can respond wholeheartedly to Buddha's profound observation. If I may paraphrase, his motives for withdrawing from society, that is, the ideals of Buddhism, could be summarized as the Three Freedoms: freedom from dogma, illusion, and greed.

Ikeda: An insightful summary, indeed. Greed, dogma, and illusion—in Buddhism, they are called *ton* (greed), *jin* (anger), and *chi* (stupidity). Buddhism is a practical philosophy aimed at seeking liberation from the iron chains of such perversions of the heart.

Ton is literally greed or avarice. *Jin* stands for anger, but rather than simple anger, it is more like a destructive impulse which drives us to so detest the existence of another that we want to annihilate them altogether. It is the most abominable kind of self-righteous dogmatism.

Chi can be translated as either stupidity or ignorance. It means the inability to correctly perceive things as they are, which in turn gives rise to distorted or twisted understanding. Rather than lack of comprehension, *chi* should be taken as misunderstanding, illusion, or misperception.

In Buddhism they are known as the Three Poisons, or essential evils lurking deep in the heart. Seeing how they corroded society, Shakyamuni left the royal palace in search of ways to overcome these evils.

Tehranian: Sufi ideals also envision freedom from the same three evils. A spiritual movement influenced by Buddhism, Sufism was a reaction against the positivism, formalism, and legalism of dogmatic Islam. It began as a quest for "freedom from dogma".

That was in contrast to the interpretation of some dogmatic theologians who insisted that the Shari'a (Islamic Divine Law) demanded rigid adherence to the letter of the Law.

Ikeda: And the Sufi Tariqa (the Way) emphasized loyalty to the spirit of the Law, didn't it?

Dogmatic adherence to the wording of the scripture, instead of concern for the original intention of the teaching and the hopes that inspired the prophet or teacher in the first place, would end up producing no more than a religion for its own sake. Religion must exist for the sake of humanity; otherwise it degenerates into narrow-minded fanaticism and dogmatism.

In the Sufi tradition, on the other hand, the way I see it, the in-depth meaning of the teaching is what matters most, not just its wording.

Tehranian: Exactly. As in most other world religions, the tensions between legalists and spiritualists have been constantly present in Islam. Rùmi, the 13th-century Sufi poet, put it starkly when he wrote,

> We have picked the marrow of the Koran,
> and thrown away the bones to the dogs.

In contemporary Iran, for instance, two leading Muslim philosophers by the names of Ali Shariati and Abdul-karim Soroush have valiantly fought against clerical dogmatism.

Ikeda: Nichiren, whose teachings we at Soka Gakkai follow, criticized clergy who could not shake their preoccupation with the superficial letter of the sutras as "priests who concentrate on the written word". This is not to say, of course, that the words in the sutras are unimportant. They must be given due respect, but obstinate adherence to the surface meaning of the word is altogether too likely to lead to the worst kind of fundamentalism. Moreover, there are problems of translation, since so many people rely on scriptural text translated from the original or from another language. Also, any language itself changes over time, from one era to another.

Nichiren figures prominently in the history of Japanese Buddhism by virtue of his keen awareness of these problems and his emphasis on the meaning, rather than wording, of sutra text. He was reaching for the spirit of the Buddha's teaching, rather than the letter.

Tehranian: Nichiren's criticism is legitimate and his approach valid. The problem boils down to one of text, meaning, and intent.

As for freedom from illusion, Sufism, like Buddhism, distinguishes between truth and illusory perceptions, a distinction that Plato, Aristotle, and later Kant all recognized in their theories of knowledge. The distinction between *zahir* (surface truth) and *batin* (inner truth) is central to the Sufi view. It takes long spiritual education to go beyond surface truths.

Ikeda: The Buddhist terms equivalent to "illusion" or "illusory perceptions" are *mythya-jòana* in Sanskrit and *hsieh-chien* (*xie-jian*) in Chinese, which literally mean "wrong views". The opposite is *tattva-jòana* and *chèng-chien* (*zheng-jian*), meaning "right views". A passage in the Lotus Sutra that reads, "The Thus Come One perceives the true aspect of the threefold world exactly as it is", presents another way to express the same idea.

You brought up Plato, Aristotle, and Kant in connection with the distinction between true and illusory perceptions, but I believe there are considerable differences among their theories of knowledge.

Tehranian: That is correct, and I will go into it further. First let me introduce the Platonic view.

In *The Republic*, using the allegory of the cave, Plato compared the human condition to that of a group of prisoners chained inside a dark cave. They are able to see only the shadows of what goes on outside reflected on the wall from an opening behind them. Plato thus distinguished between the sensory perceptions of those chained inside the cave and direct encounter with the light outside the cave.

Ikeda: The enchained prisoners could see only the shadows, which they took for reality itself. Plato's point was that the prisoners are we ourselves, ordinary people who live in real-world society. He was saying, in effect, that whatever we see in our daily lives is nothing but an illusion.

Tehranian: Sensory perceptions often mislead us. The "chains" in this allegory stand for ignorance. Only those who could free themselves from the chains of their ignorance could walk away from their illusory perceptions to encounter pure light outside the cave. Plato called them "philosopher kings", people fit to rule his ideal republic. He considered the light to be in the realm of ideas encompassing Truth, Beauty, and Goodness.

Ikeda: The so-called *Ideenlehre* of Plato. While the prison represents the realm of our daily life, the world of sunlight is the realm where reason is dominant, that is, the realm of ideas.

Tehranian: I interpret Platonic Ideas as conceptions embedded in our languages. Plato contrasted perception with conception, seeing them as the twin sources of human knowledge, but in the Platonic view, conceptions were clearly a superior source.

Ikeda: Conception is the realm of our thinking where reason governs. Plato regarded it as superior to perception because reason enables us to understand the realm of ideas.

Tehranian: The Platonic doctrine of the soul reinforced this point of view.

Ikeda: You mean Plato's doctrine of recollection (*anamnèsis*) ...

Tehranian: Yes. He proposed that we come from another world, a world of perfection with perfect knowledge, but in descending into this world, we forgot our origins. For him, therefore, learning was a process of remembering what we had forgotten. That is why his pedagogical method was dialogue—Platonic dialogue—which he employed to prod his students by means of questions to remember what their souls had lost.

Ikeda: In my conversations with young people, we often talk about Socrates and Plato, their lives and ideas. Partly because of that, I read Plato from time to time. His doctrine of *anamnèsis* is developed in *Menon*. This work contains one passage that I always find inspiring: "There is nothing that the soul has not learned." I think it is a marvelous statement that declares his belief in human potential.

Strictly speaking, the concept of *anamnèsis* is based on the idea of the eternal soul. From the point of view of Buddhism, which does not recognize the existence of such a substantive entity as the soul, the Platonic concept may seem odd, but if we interpret it as a confirmation of the infinity of human potential rather than the immortality of *psychè*, it makes a lot of sense.

Tehranian: I fully agree. My contention is that the human potential for learning is infinite. However, we are trapped by our cultural constructs (conceptions) and fivefold sense experiences (perception). We need our intuition (spiritual understanding) as well as action (trial and error) to proceed toward greater understanding.

Ikeda: To illustrate how great human potential is, the number of possible neural connections that can be made across synapses in the cerebral cortex, the seat of memory and other higher cognitive functions, is thought to be more than 10 to the 100,000th power. Compare that with the total number of positrons in the entire universe, which is estimated at less than 10 to the 100th power. Thus, figuratively speaking, the human potential outstrips what positrons can do in the universe. Suppose someone says, "My memory is only one-ten thousandth of the average memory". That would mean a memory whose power is smaller than average by only four zeros out of an approximate total of 100,000 zeros.

Tehranian: That's nothing!

Ikeda: Right. The human potential is virtually unlimited. Plato compared average people to prisoners bound by chains of ignorance. By ignorance, however, he did not mean absence of knowledge from the start, but lapse in memory of knowledge already possessed. It follows that if we can recall our originally noble nature, we can break out of the chains of ignorance.

As I see it, the lethargy and apathy that so many people experience come from lack of confidence in and conviction about the greatness of human potential.

Tehranian: I agree. People of our time are longing for a new civilization that can bring the unlimited human potential into full bloom. In the process, I think Plato, Kant, as well as the wisdom of Buddhism and Islam, among many others, will have very large roles to play.

Now, Aristotle accepted the proposition of Plato, his mentor, though only partially. Aristotle believed in the primacy of perception (sense experiences) as a source of knowledge. That's why he is considered the founding philosopher of modern science.

Ikeda: You mean his distinction between conception and sensory perception, between the realm of ideas and that of reality.

Tehranian: Immanuel Kant (1724–1804), the founding father of modern philosophy, took this theory of knowledge a few steps further. He distinguished between the noumenal and phenomenal worlds. By noumenal world, he meant the world of "names". We name the world in order to understand it. Categorizing things by name is how we make the world knowable.

Ikeda: You have concisely and clearly outlined how, in the history of philosophy, analyses of the way the human mind works became increasingly more sophisticated and precise over the centuries. In a way, though, Plato and Kant stand on opposite sides in their theories of knowledge. For Plato, the world understood by reason was the realm of ideas, an ideal world. He considered logos and understanding through reason superior to sensory perceptions.

Tehranian: Whereas in Kant reason does not take precedence …

Ikeda: Right. Kant was explicit in recognizing the limitations on human intellect and understanding, *Verstand* in his terminology. He believed that much is simply beyond human powers and that it was sheer arrogance to assume that we are capable of understanding everything through logic and reason.

In our own time, we have seen the modern cult of instrumental reason give birth to tragedies as monstrous as Auschwitz and Hiroshima. Knowing of these awful events, it is not difficult for us to understand the grounds for Kant's critique of *Verstand*. Because he fully grasped the limitations of *Verstand*, Kant could see how views and philosophies that were constructed on the premise of human intellect and understanding alone would eventually descend into dogmatism.

Tehranian: In that sense, we should say, perhaps, that in his critique of dogmatism Kant was an untiring seeker of the conditions for "open dialogue" that you and I are seeking.

To be sure, human beings are not capable of knowing the true essence of things or phenomena, and yet we must keep seeking that which is sublime, the eternal. As long as we are engaged in this search, Kant believed, we can maintain our freedom. His position is in line with the orientation of our own dialogue. Human knowledge is limited by time and space. Only through dialogue can we expand that time and space.

Ikeda: I agree. Kant's spirit is the same religious spirit we talked about that seeks that which is eternal.

Let me, at this point, elaborate on the similarities between Buddhism and the Kantian theory of knowledge. By reason alone, we cannot know the thing itself (*Ding an sich*)—that which is noumenal. So we give names to things to distinguish them and make them intelligible. "Man" and "woman", "friend" and "foe", or "Muslim" and "Christian" are appellations coined to categorize people and make them knowable, but they are not the same as individual human beings, each with his or her own identity. Kant was very clear in pointing out this pitfall in the way the mind works when it blurs that distinction.

That is exactly what Buddhism does. As we have discussed before, Shakyamuni and Nagarjuna, among others, were severe critics of conceptual perception and knowledge gained via language. On this particular point, therefore, Buddhism bears a closer resemblance to Kant, coming some twenty centuries later, than to the contemporary philosopher Plato.

Tehranian: That is one of the remarkable strengths of Buddhism. All the dichotomies people often use—good and evil, light and darkness, black and white, democracy and dictatorship, for example—illustrate how our limited minds define the world. Buddhism definitely suggested the inadequacy of such an approach. Dichotomous thinking is the most primitive form of categorizing the world.

Ikeda: People simplify and categorize the diverse, multifaceted world, being unable to perceive it as it is. And they put themselves on the side of goodness, light, white, and democracy.

Tehranian: In that sense, we are all hostage to language in our search for truth. In our search for truth, we must go beyond language to music, visual arts, religious rituals, and even silence.

Ikeda: Subjective elements and prejudices creep into what we are certain is "objective" reality. We should never arbitrarily assume that poor people, for example, are "not well educated" or "ill-mannered". For financial or other reasons, they might not have received advanced education, but the amount of formal schooling one has received and his or her personal character are two different things.

I know of many craftsmen who have worked assiduously with their hands for years. It is often the case that they are men of finer character than some people with degrees from famous universities. These craftsmen might not have much formal education, but they have learned a lot from experience.

Tehranian: I could not agree more. *Vox populi, vox dei*, the voice of the people is the voice of God. That is why despite its shortcomings, democracy is the best form of government.

Ikeda: The Buddhist concept of *ku* (Skt., *shūnya* or *shūnyatā*) is an insistent call for attention to our own proclivity to become trapped in "fabricated objectivity" and "wrong views", and it prompts us to look toward "right views" and perceive the true aspect of phenomena exactly as they are.

Tehranian: I am familiar with the concept.

Ikeda: The term *ku* (non-substantiality, void, emptiness) is often thought—wrongly—by Japanese to have a nihilistic connotation. According to the theory of *ku*, the words and concepts we take for granted are actually synthetic artifacts created out of human imagination and habit. Such earthly things as are made out of human contrivance are called *gyo* (Skt., *samskara*) in Buddhism. "All [worldly] things flow and nothing is permanent" is one of the basic Buddhist teachings. It was to help free us from the "chains of habit" that Shakyamuni and Nagarjuna developed some of their most powerful philosophies.

Tehranian: From the Kantian point of view, every thought intended for speech loses its validity at the moment of its utterance. Reality is in constant flux, yet language petrifies. From a Sufi perspective, poverty (*faqr*) or nothingness (*fana*) is the highest level of spiritual achievement. Symbolically, this means liberation from worldly possessions and preoccupations in order to dissolve the self into the eternal.

Ikeda: Reality is an endless series of changes, impossible to bind with ossified words, consciousness, or concepts. To become hostage to language is to lose sight of the essence of things. The Buddhist term *shoho jisso* (true aspect of all phenomena) conveys this idea well, referring to the changing reality of things.

Tehranian: Two of Rùmi's couplets go right to the heart of what we are talking about:

> Whoever has been taught the secrets of love,
> His mouth is sealed, his lips are sewn.

> Conflict among people is born of semantics;
> As we move deeper into essence, harmony shall reign.

Ikeda: Needless to say, there is no dialogue without language. We must always take care, however, to resist being captivated by language and to stay free of obsession with words. Only then will we be able to gain the wisdom to perceive things as they are and speak the truth.

"His mouth is sealed", wrote Rùmi, but he did not keep his own mouth shut. He was a poet, a genius of words. But his warning against the "petrification" of words is still valid.

Tehranian: Yes, this is so. We must always try to go deeper.

What I have called the Third Freedom, freedom from greed, is of course central to the Buddhist path. In Buddhist teaching greed is one of the major sources of human suffering, and suffering will not end until and unless we learn to overcome our possessive attitudes toward people and things. But greed can be focused on wealth, power, formal knowledge, or longevity.

Ikeda: A great many people in our time are under the illusion that satisfying their desires is what they live for.

Tehranian: In our acquisitive societies, we are constantly bombarded by commercial advertising that induces false needs and real appetites. Our personal identities are thus socially defined by our habits of consumption. We have a fetish of consuming identities.

Ikeda: It is truly pathetic. To think that individuality, that precious, irreplaceable gift, can now be expressed by choice of products.

Tehranian: The car we drive, the perfume we wear, the celebrities with whom we try to associate—these things determine our fabricated identity. But in this rat race, the more we have, the less we are. Our consumer identity rests on our external possessions rather than our inner personal life. This may be part of what T.S. Eliot meant when he wrote his haunting poem, "The Hollow Men", which begins,

> We are Hollow Men
> We are stuffed men.

Gandhi best expressed the implications of increasingly acquisitive societies when he observed that, "There is enough in the world for everyone's need; there is not enough for everyone's greed".

Ikeda: Once the devil whispered to Shakyamuni, "If you were to abandon Buddhist practice, you would be able to amass a fortune as big as the Himalayas". To that, Shakyamuni resolutely declared, "Even if you were to turn the Himalayas into gold, and even if you were then to double that, it would not satisfy the desires of but a single person. People should know this truth and, accordingly, restrain their conduct" (*Samyutta-Nikaya*, 4.20).

There are no beautiful highlands, crystal lakes, or chirping birds in the Himalayan mountains of greed. Today, when acquisitiveness seems to have gained unprecedented power, it is more important than ever for people to control their desires and free themselves of greed.

Tehranian: It is indeed. The Sufi poet Sa'adi puts it this way, "The greedy eyes can be filled either with abstinence or the grave's ashes."

Ikeda: Right now the storm of the globally intertwined market economy is raging, packing enough power to knock out a country's fiscal and financial systems in a week.

Tehranian: That is just what the market economy is, a storm whose intensity keeps right in step with the frenzy for consumption and acquisition. The Toda Institute's report on reforming global governance, entitled *Reimagining the World: Toward Democratic Governance*, has outlived some concrete proposals to remedy the situation. The longer version of the book has been published under the title of *Democratizing Global Governance*.

Economics for People

Ikeda: Good, the world is thus not without light. I think there is a large ray of hope for the future in a new trend now emerging. Let me quote a few lines from Tagore:

> I would rather look forward to the opening of a new chapter in humankind's history after the cataclysm is over and the atmosphere rendered clean with the spirit of service and sacrifice. Perhaps that dawn comes from this horizon, from the East where the sun rises.

I truly believe that new wisdom and a new framework for action are emerging from the peripheral areas of the free market and economies based on high mass consumption. One indication of the new trend is the thinking of Professor Amartya Sen, which is clearly making an impact, for he was awarded the Nobel Prize in economics in 1998, when market activity was already turning into a worldwide tempest.

Tehranian: Dr. Sen is an outstanding thinker. He is the first Asian Nobel laureate in economics, and he did it by injecting, theoretically, the idea of human potential into the framework of economics, which until now has been focused on the quest for utility.

Ikeda: Actually, he was born in Santiniketan, in the outskirts of Calcutta, where Tagore founded a university whose basic philosophy was centered on the ideal of "whole-person education". Dr. Sen's first name, Amartya, is said to have been given him by Tagore. I believe it means "beyond death", or "immortality".

Tehranian: In his economic theory, Dr. Sen gives more weight to freedom than to assets and economic efficiency. In this, it is said, he is giving concrete expression to Tagore's message to humanity—that people must cast off their preconceptions, habits, assumptions, so that they can be completely free to exhibit their own creativity.

Ikeda: Dr. Sen's unchanging position that "to allow injustice is tantamount to doing injustice" has also had a strong impact. That standpoint is identical to the ideas of Tsunesaburo Makiguchi. Convinced that to do nothing about evil when you see it around you is the same thing as committing evil yourself, our founding president squarely confronted the militarist regime and religious authorities that cooperated in the war effort.

Tehranian: He was a remarkable man. I have always felt nothing but admiration for Mr. Makiguchi.

Ikeda: Dr. Sen acknowledged in a press interview that he is indebted to Tagore for his uncompromising stand against injustice (*Tokyo Shimbun*, January 1, 1999).

While the advanced industrial countries claim that they are not responsible for poverty and famine in the Third World, except when their policies and actions happened to be the direct cause of such troubles, Dr. Sen counters with the following proposition: The question before us now is not whether you have done injustice, but what you can do to deal with a situation and rectify injustice.

Tehranian: In our world, that is indeed a startling proposition.

Ikeda: "Commitment" is another of Dr. Sen's original ideas. In the sense he uses it, to have commitment is to view the suffering of others as injustice and to sacrifice oneself to eliminate that injustice. As a general rule, economic activities are expected to produce some kind of profit for someone. In Dr. Sen's theory of commitment, however, one of the axioms of economic activity is the pursuit of "losing" in the form of self-sacrifice.

Tehranian: Dr. Sen himself lived through the 1943 famine in Bengal, which took three million lives. It was that experience, I understand, that motivated him later to call for "ethics in economic activities". His theory provides a powerful rationale for economic assistance to developing countries.

Ikeda: That was important. And while Dr. Sen is clearly very well-versed in Western scholarship—he has made, I believe, a fundamental reappraisal of the classical economic theories of Adam Smith—I feel certain that Tagore's philosophy influenced his approach to economics in a very fundamental way. The spirit of Tagore and Gandhi will never grow old.

Tehranian: The same is true of the thought of Buddha and Muhammad. Islam, as you know, is etymologically related to *Salaam* (peace) in Arabic and *Shalom* in Hebrew. It can be interpreted as what you've called Active Peace (Ikeda Peace Proposal, Jan., 2000). Active peace cannot be achieved without social justice.

Ikeda: Absolutely. They all provided a rich reservoir of ideas that continue to provide new knowledge and inspiration. They are like spiritual fountains that never dry up.

There is another Asian economist whose theories are attracting wide attention, and that is Dr. Muhammad Yunus of Bangladesh, who is perhaps best known for his innovative microcredit lending system. He is the founding president of the Grameen Bank.

Tehranian: Dr. Sen's theory is called the "economics of the poor", while Dr. Yunus' bank is known as the "bank for the poor". Both derive their rationale from the need to find ways for the poor to overcome their poverty, not for ways to let the rich amass more wealth.

Ikeda: The microcredit system of providing small, unsecured loans was first implemented in Bangladesh, Dr. Yunus' home country.

Tehranian: That's right. It provides poor people who have no collateral with small loans. Before finalizing a loan, someone from the bank visits the area where the loan applicant lives and talks with that person, his/her family, friends, and others in the community to determine what might be the most suitable business for the applicant. The Toda Institute has proposed to create a series of global banks, trusts, and funds to provide low interest loans to poor women, minorities, peasants, and small businesses to encourage self-help and indigenous development.

Ikeda: This is dialogue in action. It is also localism working at its best. Armchair theories may be elegant, but they accomplish nothing on the ground and cannot lead us to practicable solutions for real, immediate problems.

At first, the idea of micro-credit was considered to be a will-o'-the-wisp. The sceptics thought it was crazy to even consider lending money to the poor. "They will borrow as much as they can lay their hands on, and pay back almost nothing" was a sentiment voiced frequently. What has happened, however, has totally confounded that expectation: so far the rate of debt default is under one percent.

Tehranian: Over 99 percent repayment rate—that is astounding!

Ikeda: To discover that someone is willing to loan them money despite their impoverished state has given a real boost to the self-confidence of those people. They are encouraged by a new sense of being trusted and being needed by society. That confidence has sustained the hard efforts they invest to make their enterprises work.

The whole experience with microcredit has demonstrated that people are by nature good, wise, and honest. What better evidence do we need? I think microcredit's approach and record of accomplishments can serve as a model for international economic assistance in the future. Its basic premise is not to provide aid to the poor from above, but to work with the people in each case to examine the causes of their poverty and together find ways to overcome them.

Tehranian: In Bangladesh alone, as many as 12 million people are working hard to rise out of poverty with the support of microcredit loans. Microcredit is also operating in about sixty other countries, including South Africa and countries in Europe and the Americas, as a part of programs to help the poor.

Ikeda: An undertaking like this might be called "human rights economics" or the "economics of compassion". It is highly significant that this trend in economic thinking, which is so very different from economic theories based on instrumental rationalism, has emerged at just the moment when modern rationalism in the form of free market economics is raging all over the world.

Tehranian: Which takes us right back to Tagore's words that you quoted earlier! Some Islamic thinkers such as Ali Shariati and Morteza Mottaheri have also written extensively on economics of unity (*eqtesad towhidi*) emphasizing compassion and social justice.

Ikeda: Dr. Yunus appears to be critical of conservative religious institutions, but his autobiography shows that he was raised in a very pious Muslim family and influenced by people who burned with lofty religious ideals.

I understand that they chant prayers from the Koran during the anniversary celebrations of the Grameen Bank's founding. In any case, Dr. Yunus' endeavor is certainly keeping the Koranic commandment to help widows and the poor very much alive.

I have said this before, but I really think we need to give more serious recognition to the value of the suq or bazaar, the marketplace found in all traditional Islamic communities. It has much to offer that is totally lost in the financial market, where millions of dollars are transacted at the touch of a keyboard.

Tehranian: The Islamic market place is alive. There, you can see the faces of people, you can hear their exchanges. You can feel their very breathing. When I visited Central Asia in 1992, 1994 and 1996, I was struck by the fact that 70 years of Soviet domination had not been able to destroy the traditional bazaars that were the old part of the Central Asian economies that showed every sign of vitality. In the outskirts of Ashkabad, I witnessed a flea market at which thousands of people were exchanging their goods, ranging from jewelry, textile and carpets to auto parts and domesticated animals. By contrast, the government stores were empty of people and goods. Markets are indispensable but they should be free of monopolies and exploitations.

Ikeda: An early monograph by the symbolic anthropologist Clifford Geertz was a detailed analysis of the suq. His discussion of the lack of fixed prices, one of the unique features of the suq, was extremely perceptive. Prices vary, apparently, depending on the relationship between the merchant and the customer.

Tehranian: His view is quite different from the typically biased Orientalist image of predatory, cunning merchants out to bilk tourists of their last dime. The fixed prices of modern department stores give the consumers no room to maneuver.

Ikeda: To the contrary, Geertz found in the suq a system of social transactions that supersede relationships governed by greed, with one side trying to wring as much money as possible from the sale and the other trying to hand over as little as possible. According to Geertz, the suq is not a place where fraud-vs.-sucker games are played out. Geertz's research, which was pioneering work in Western scholarship, prompted growing numbers of researchers in several disciplines to study the suq economy. William Davis, for example, considers the essence of the suq economy to consist of some of the best human qualities: trust, morality, sincerity, and altruism.

Tehranian: Suq merchants keep their shops in the open market. If they always charged unreasonable prices, they would not last very long. They are perfectly aware that in order to stay in business and retain a loyal clientele, they have to be fair and generous to a point. In haggling over prices, friendships are made while reaching a level acceptable to both buyer and seller.

Ikeda: To people accustomed to the terms of the capitalist free market, the suq's lack of fixed prices may invoke images of a feeble economy and precarious human relationships, but such images do not take into account the vigorous, long-term relationships that the suq embodies and sustains, relationships that keep the society strong and vital.

Tehranian: The suq economy is living proof of the viability of an economic system that is miles apart from the basic assumptions of modern economics, namely, the pursuit of profit and accumulation of capital.

Ikeda: In the economy of the suq we can see the undeniable presence of truly human values that attach more importance to positive relationships than to calculated gain and profitable sales.

The Persian poet Mosleh al-Din Sa'adi (ca. 1184–1291) has a merchant in Gulistan [*The Rose Garden*] say,

> I want to carry Persian brimstone to China, where I have heard it bears a very high price; from thence I will transport China ware to Greece, and take the brocades of Greece to India, and Indian steel to Aleppo. The glassware of Aleppo I will convey to Yemen, and from thence go with striped clothes to Persia; after which I will leave off trade and sit down in my shop. (Translated by Reuben Levy, p. 171)

For this merchant, the entrepreneurial life is a happy one, filled with rich cross-cultural encounters. His success in business does not require an ever-expanding scale of operations, but simply opening a small shop in the suq where he can bargain face-to-face with his customers.

Tehranian: That kind of life is qualitatively different from a life characterized by ceaselessly multiplying desires. As you know, Sa'adi himself traveled widely through Asia! He engaged in many professions, including brick laying in Damascus. His wisdom was gained through practical experience. His volumes *Gulistan* and *Bustan* (*Rose Garden* and *Meadows*) became the bibles of the Islamic world from New Delhi to Samarkand and Istanbul.

Ikeda: There is nothing left of humanity in the big financial markets. Certainly the flip-flops of stock prices and exchange rates produce the gamut of emotions, from exuberant joy to despair, but the transactions themselves are devoid of any interplay between human hearts.

Tehranian: You are right, and "humanity" is the key word here. It is the common thread in Dr. Sen's pioneering economic theory and Dr. Yunus' novel concept and application of microcredit. And it dominates the suq, also, where the faces of humans are what sustain it.

Ikeda: It really is time to bring in an economic system that can work to erase expressions of misery and agony from people's faces and replace them with joy and gratification—an "economics of happiness".

Human Rights and Buddhism

Tehranian: I have learned a great deal from you about the many facets of Buddhism and what it stands for in the realms of both ideas and action. We can be certain, I think, that Buddhism will play a major role in making the 21st century a "century of humanity".

I can think of no more persuasive way to demonstrate the relevance of Buddhist principles than to cite the human rights movement. The world has gone through a long journey in this quest, and we have made some progress, but we have not yet come within reach of fulfilling Buddha's vision of human compassion.

Ikeda: I am constantly impressed with your knowledge and appreciation of Buddhism.

Tehranian: In modern Europe, human rights first focused on what came to be called natural rights, that is, "life, liberty, and the pursuit of happiness". They reflect ideas that came to fruition during the Enlightenment in Europe and became the basis for the founding credo of the United States—the Declaration of Independence—and other landmark documents.

Ikeda: Those are the first generation of human rights, aren't they? The right to life was the basic minimum human right to live unthreatened by a despotic monarch. Not even this most fundamental right was honored in premodern Europe or elsewhere.

Tehranian: The second generation was instituted in the Universal Declaration of Human Rights, which focused primarily on individual civil and political rights, chiefly freedom of thought, speech, conscience, assembly, and petition.

In response to pressure from socialist countries, where social and economic rights were emphasized, the rights of employment, social security, labor strikes, compensatory hiring, and social welfare were later incorporated into the Declaration of Social and Economic Rights. Together, the three documents are known as the International Bill of Human Rights.

Ikeda: In *Zur Judenfrage* [On the Question of the Jews] (1844), Karl Marx attacked the idea of individual human rights as a sure guarantee of self-concern that would undermine society. He wrote that, "They are nothing but rights held by members of a bourgeois society, which is to say rights of selfish individuals, rights of those detached from humanity and the community." Clearly Marx saw individual rights as something that only the bourgeoisie would ever enjoy.

Marx posited the idea of civil rights, or individual rights of a single member of civil society, which probably fall into the category of second-generation human rights.

Tehranian: That is correct. The third generation of rights came to be recognized primarily through the struggles of colonized peoples who saw a threat to their own collective cultural life in the cultural domination by the industrialized countries. Whereas the first and second generations of rights were primarily concerned with individuals, the third generation recognized the rights of collectivities. This has led to a series of collective rights such as those of women, minorities, and children, and against any form of racial discrimination and genocide. The three generations of rights are mutually reinforcing.

Ikeda: It is quite a progression—from the basic right of individual existence to social rights, and then on to cultural rights.

Tehranian: Exactly. And now, in association with the environmentalist movement, a fourth generation of human rights has entered into the international discourse. In contrast to the first, second, and third generations of rights, which focus on humans, the new generation of rights may be described as inter-species.

Ikeda: The scope of "rights" has been widening from individuals, to society, and now to the non-human parts of nature.

Tehranian: Think of the scale of the man-made environmental disasters of the last few decades; Chernobyl, Three-Mile Island, Bhopal, Exxon Valdez, the burning of the Kuwaiti oil wells ...

Ikeda: These accidents are catastrophic in both time and space. They damage not only the current generation, but leave deadly effects that will remain far into the future, and ranging far and wide they spread misery indiscriminately across political and geographic boundaries. At this rate, all we will bequeath to future generations is liabilities. We must not let that happen. A top-priority item on the agenda of all nations for the next few years should be to examine what possible legacies and what assets we can leave for our offspring.

Tehranian: Those disasters, plus an increasing appreciation of the wisdom of ancient indigenous cultures—until recently denigrated by industrial societies as "primitive" and so forth—have brought home the fact that humanity cannot survive, let alone prosper, without a living earth, sky, oceans, and the multitudes of different plants and animals. The hubris of the Enlightenment project, putting humans above and in control of nature, is at last being challenged by an environmentalist view that places humans in nature as one part of it.

Ikeda: The growing strength of that view is deeply indebted to the thinking of the native peoples of the Americas and elsewhere, the aboriginal peoples of Oceania, and the ideas in Islamic, Buddhist, and Hindu philosophies, as well as other idea systems from the Third World.

Tehranian: That is so true. And those ideas are all related to the fourth generation of rights, which focus on the interdependency of species and everything in the natural world. They seem very closely tied in with the Buddhist concept of dependent origination.

Yet we still need a fifth generation that could move the focus away from human rights onto human caring and compassion. It would mean shifting discourse from rights to responsibilities, from legal precepts to social obligations, from the letter of the law to the spirit of the law, from minds to hearts.

Ikeda: You have made this point very well and have explained the history of human rights in a clear, coherent way. I myself feel strongly that the discourse on human rights as they have developed over the centuries is now approaching the level of the teachings of the world religions, including Shakyamuni's idea of compassion.

The fifth generation of rights that you suggest is something to be respectfully seen in someone else rather than in oneself. Seen in that way, I believe the fifth generation has a strong affinity with the Buddhist idea of compassion.

Let me relate an anecdote from one of the sutras that brings out the Buddhist idea of human rights. One day Shakyamuni encounters a sick person. He bathes the person's body with a cloth, washes the dirty bedding, and dries it in the sun. Shakyamuni then tells his disciples that, "Helping the sick is the same thing as serving the Buddha".

Tehranian: What the sutra is saying, then, is that compassion does not mean giving alms or doing something charitable for someone below you, but acting for that person out of a feeling of respect.

Ikeda: Because to show compassion is to venerate the Buddha, if anything it expresses a sense of doing service for someone greater than yourself. In Buddhism, therefore, an altruistic act is considered a practice that elevates oneself.

Tehranian: That makes a lot of sense. It is a really noble way of thinking. I agree that the Buddhist concept of compassion could become the guiding principle for the fifth generation of human rights.

Perspectives on Eternal Life

Ikeda: It is generally believed that Buddhism is quite different from Islam in its view of life and death.

Tehranian: Yes. While Buddhist teaching clearly affirms transmigration, Islam, like Christianity and Judaism, expounds the view that we are born into this world but once and after death we wait for the last judgment.

Ikeda: Let us develop that subject for a moment—the differences between the two religions.

Tehranian: To start with my conclusion first, the two religions have numerous superficial differences, but if we pay close attention to the symbolic meaning of their teachings, they have fundamental similarities.

Ikeda: Let me say a few words about the Buddhist view of life and death. Among the oldest Buddhist sutras are a pair entitled *Theragatha* and *Therigatha*. "Thera-" means male disciples and "theri-" means female disciples. The two sutras consist of collected testimonials by Shakyamuni's followers. They offer a vivid picture of how those people lived and what their afflictions were before they became Buddhist believers.

Tehranian: They contain accounts of actual experiences of the Buddha's disciples?

Ikeda: Yes. The accounts tell how the disciples were healed of their suffering, whether from sickness or poverty, or separation from parents, children, or loved ones, after their encounter with Shakyamuni. Reading *Theragatha* and *Therigatha* makes you realize how many followers attained the state of immortality after embracing Buddhism. Both sutras make frequent reference to that.

Tehranian: Could you give some examples?

Ikeda: In one case, a female disciple writes, "I lost my whole clan, I lost my husband, and while I was ridiculed by the people in society, I found the way leading to immortality. I mastered the noble eight-fold path bringing me to immortality" (*Therigatha*, sections 221 and 222). Another passage from the same sutra reads, "This is the state of being ever-young, this is immortality, this is the state of being ever-young and immortal. To be in this state is to be free from worries, enemies, obstructions, errors, fears, and burning pain" (Ibid., section 513).

Tehranian: In other words, the ideal state expounded by Shakyamuni Buddha was described by his disciples as a "state of being immortal".

Ikeda: Precisely. Shakyamuni himself used the word immortality. Even during the period when he was beginning to propagate his teaching, he declared, "The gate to immortality has opened" (*Vinaya-pitaka*, The Great Chapter, V, 12). And, "The drum of immortality shall sound in the world of darkness" (Ibid., VI, 8).

It is important to understand exactly what is meant by "immortality" here. It could not possibly refer literally to some kind of physical immunity to old age and death.

Tehranian: Of course it couldn't. Gautama Buddha himself actually died.

Ikeda: Buddhism also does not accept the immortality of the soul, or the idea that the body is a vessel for the soul and after death the soul departs from the body and moves to another body. In short, immortality here does not mean immortality of the soul.

Similarly, the doctrine of reincarnation should not be taken literally. The important thing is how belief in that doctrine can change one's outlook and life for the better.

Tehranian: That is an important point. The Buddhist idea, really a myth, of reincarnation or transmigration teaches us not about the immortality of the soul, but how to consider ourselves as part of nature, rather than detached from and above nature. Myths impart profound truths if not taken literally.

Ikeda: That is a good way to express it. For example, looking at a bird flying among the trees, perhaps you wonder if he could have been your relative in a previous lifetime. Or you see a dog right there beside you, and ponder the chance that she may be a bodhisattva who chose the hard life of a dog for ascetic practice. If you think that way, you will never scorn or mistreat birds or dogs. Whether they were in fact your relatives or are bodhisattvas in practice does not matter; your conviction that other creatures are indeed reincarnations will change the way you live.

Suppose you were born into very difficult circumstances. If you can believe that you have chosen your particular life because you vowed in your previous lifetime to try to save people with similar hardships, then the way you live will become more positive and more constructive.

Tehranian: That is true. I understand your point very well. The idea of reincarnation taken symbolically should lead us to revere every living form as a possible relative, and to confront suffering with courage.

But the same idea has its dangers, too. If taken literally, the reincarnation myth can lead to the legitimization of rigid caste systems and gross social injustice.

Ikeda: You are so right. Brahmanism, in fact, took the idea of reincarnation literally. Giving full credence to the doctrine of transmigration, Brahmans argued that one's social status was determined by one's karma in previous existences. People of lowly status had only themselves to blame, not society, for their plight.

Tehranian: Myths are easily transformed into ideologies of power legitimizing a particular type of oppression, such as the caste system.

In contrast to Buddhism, which proclaims no doctrine of the soul, the Abrahamic religions presuppose a body and a soul for human beings. Although the body perishes, the soul lives on forever. But as I said earlier, despite superficial differences in terminology, the Abrahamic doctrine of the soul is not fundamentally different from the Buddhist doctrine of reincarnation in its deepest meaning. Human souls await their fate in purgatory until the Judgement Day when good and evil deeds are evaluated. Depending on one's lifetime behavior, the soul ends in Heaven or Hell. This myth can be interpreted to mean that we live here and now in heaven or hell, happiness or misery, depending on how we behave.

Ikeda: Immortality does not mean the negation of death, but freedom from suffering and liberation from the karmic cycle of reincarnation. This idea is expressed well in the Lotus Sutra. The sixteenth chapter is entitled "The Life Span of the Thus Come One", in which we are told that Shakyamuni was Buddha from the infinite past.

Tehranian: Of course that is not meant to be taken literally. Its meaning is symbolic, isn't it?

Ikeda: That's right. Referring to this principle, Nichiren stated, "Because this is the eternal and immutable Buddha in his original state, he exists just as he always has" (*Gosho*, p. 759). What that means is that "Buddha of the infinite past" is not something you can find by going back to the past, but something you can manifest in your heart now, by practicing the way of Buddhism.

Tehranian: If we can see ourselves as part of an eternal cosmos, as indeed we are, we will be liberated from the anxieties that turn into fear of death and greed. Then we can devote ourselves more faithfully to serving others. The happiness of others will become our own happiness. Whether we call this eternal spirit Yahweh, Jesus, Allah, or Buddha, by participating in the eternal, we too become immortal.

Ikeda: Shakyamuni said, that carrying out religious practices with diligence is the state of being immortal. "Heedfulness is the path to the Deathless. Heedlessness is the path to death. The heedful die not. The heedless are as if dead already" (*Dhamma-pada*, verse 21).

Rabindranath Tagore, whose spirit was in harmony with the Buddhist view of life, produced poetry of astounding depth and beauty. A part of one of his verses goes,

> ... the more generously I give of my life,
> the more it surges forth.
> It is inexhaustible.

Buddhism sees life and death as eternal, but it does not teach the presence of an immortal soul. What that means is that one can live eternal life within the immediate moment.

Tehranian: Our discussion reminds me of two women, Princess Diana and Mother Theresa. They both captured the hearts of the world's people by dedicating their lives to causes greater than themselves. Diana transformed herself from a future British queen to the world's Queen of Hearts by championing causes on behalf of victims of sickness, war, and other misfortune, including a campaign against murderous land mines.

Mother Theresa, whose small, frail, aged body presented a sharp contrast to Diana's youthful charm and vigor, was awarded the Nobel Peace Prize for her work among the poor of India. These two extraordinary women were vibrant examples of two spirits who conquered death by living the full potential of their lives.

They will live on in the memories of people everywhere as a princess and a saint who, instead of taking the road of indolent indifference or isolation from others, chose to devote themselves to alleviating the suffering of others.

Ikeda: Let me raise a question that has been a burning issue in the Islamic world since the creation of Israel in 1949. What do you think of the Arab-Israeli conflict? What role can dialogue play in restoring peace with justice to both sides?

Tehranian: The dialogue at the Second Camp David (July, 2000), like the First (1978), is promising. The Arab-Israeli conflict is one of the most complex and tragic in the world. It has a long history and unfortunately is not going to go away soon. Despite the general impression, this is not a religious conflict, but religious extremism has exacerbated it. Jews and Muslims lived together peacefully in West

Asia for centuries. In fact, Jews had a prominent position as scholars and administrators in the Islamic Abbasid, Ottoman, and Safavid Empires. Jewish communities were protected in Islamic societies as one of the Peoples of the Book. Jewish, Christian, and Zoroastrian communities each enjoyed considerable internal autonomy under Islamic rule.

Following Hitler's rise to power, that picture changed. As Jewish immigrants from Europe took refuge in the British mandate of Palestine, Arabs were displaced from their homes and farms. This was initially accomplished by outright purchases of land from Arab landlords by the Jewish Agency to provide settlement for the newly arrived Jewish immigrants. In the past, every time land had changed hands among Arab landlords, peasants would remain with the land. But this round, they had to move out. During the 1930s and 1940s, this process of displacement created increasing tension between the Jewish and Arab communities. Both communities were increasingly nationalistic and wished to rid themselves of the British colonial yoke. In the meantime, to obtain the cooperation of both Jews and Arabs in their war efforts, the British had promised each community a "homeland".

With the impending departure of the British, in 1947, the United Nations voted for the partition of Palestine into two Jewish and Arab states. When the British withdrew, in 1948, Israel declared its independence while the Arab states that rejected the partition attacked the new state. That was the first of four wars fought between the two sides, in 1948–49, 1956, 1967, and 1973. Given Arab disunity and Western military and political support, Israel won more territory in each of these wars.

The peace process between Arabs and Israelis began dramatically with Egyptian President Sadat's trip to Jerusalem. In 1979, Israel and Egypt signed the so-called Camp David Accords that provided for phased withdrawal of Israel from Sinai. However, the accords led to the isolation of Egypt from the Arab World. Palestinians, feeling abandoned by their most powerful Arab ally, took to guerrilla warfare in the Intifada movement. That forced Israel to agree to the Oslo Accords that brought Yitzhak Rabin and Yasser Arafat to shake hands at the American White House. The peace process initiated by this handshake has led to a bumpy road full of obstacles.

Seven critical issues remain unresolved:

- The Israeli annexation of the Golan Heights that were captured from Syria in 1967.

- The Israeli occupation of the West Bank that was captured from Jordan also in 1967.
- The Israeli unilateral declaration of Jerusalem as its capital.
- The increasing clashes between Palestinians and the new Jewish settlers in the West Bank.
- The repatriation of Palestinian refugees outside of Israel and the West Bank.
- The question of a Palestinian independent state to be established in the West Bank.
- The guarantee for mutual security for both states of Israel and Palestine.

Israel's unilateral withdrawal from southern Lebanon in 1999 has largely removed that issue from the peace agenda. But under the United States auspices, in July, 2000, the Second Camp David negotiations between Palestinian Chairman Yasser Arafat and Israeli Prime Minister Ehud Barak have had to take up all of the other thorny issues. None of them lends itself to an easy solution. The problem revolves around the continuing territorial claims of both sides for the same land. Unless leaders of both sides are willing to compromise on creative solutions, a stalemate will continue. In the meantime, hundreds if not thousands of lives are being lost in ceaseless clashes.

This is not a conflict that, as partisan views argue, pits right against wrong. It is a problem of Israeli rights against Arab rights. It is what true tragedies are made of. The road to a durable peace is to get away from blame games and the traditional notions of exclusive national sovereignty. A just solution would recognize shared sovereignty over Jerusalem—a holy city to Jews, Christians, and Muslims alike. It also would allow a new Palestinian state to control the West Bank in a federal arrangement with the state of Israel. The devil is, of course, in the details. We should leave that to seasoned peacemakers, wise mediators, and courageous politicians on both sides. Peace is a historical necessity. The last 50 years must be considered an aberration from the historical norm of peaceful co-existence of Jews, Muslims, and Christians in the Holy Lands. In this context, Palestinian suicide bombing and the unilateralist policies of U.S. President Bush and Israeli Prime Minister Sharon have exacerbated the existing conflicts.

CHAPTER 9

A Century of War

Remembering Josei Toda

Ikeda: The year 2000 marked the 100th anniversary of the birth of Josei Toda, second president of Soka Gakkai and the man who guided me until the day he died. Born in February, 1900, Toda provided a solid conceptual basis for peace policy and research that has endured, grounded in his uncompromising stand against nuclear weapons that he articulated in his manifesto of 1957, and his vision of peace and equity among the "global family", what we call transnationalism.

I understand that the Toda Institute held an international conference in February, 2000 in honor of Toda.

Tehranian: That is correct. Timed to coincide with the centennial anniversary of President Toda's birth, the February conference was planned around the theme "Dialogue Among Civilizations: A New Peace Agenda for a New Millennium".

When the Institute was launched in 1996, we charted a research program focused on the broad topic of "Human Security and Global Governance" (HUGG). By the end of 1998, we had held four international meetings, in Honolulu and London in 1997, and in Durban (South Africa) and Sydney (Australia) in 1998. The next one was held in Istanbul in March 1999, focusing on "Security and Cooperation in West Asia", and that was followed by a conference in Berlin in the autumn. The conference in February drew on the results of all the previous meetings, representing a culmination of the work we have done so far.

Ikeda: Let me say once again how deeply we appreciate the matchless personal dedication and professional skill you have brought to this project.

Tehranian: On the contrary, for me it is a privilege to be able to participate in research with goals that are so high and so important as ours. The greatest asset the Toda Institute has is the combined vision of the three successive presidents of Soka Gakkai, presidents Makiguchi, Toda, and Ikeda, who have pursued with relentless determination the dream of world unity, peace, and justice. Mr. Makiguchi's "humanitarian competition", Mr. Toda's antinuclear manifesto and concept of the "global family", and your own projects to realize those dreams through "dialogue with the world"—they all all exemplify living as true global citizens.

By building on the philosophy of global peace shared by all three presidents, I am confident that the Institute will be able to fulfill its goal of promoting the global citizenship demanded by the 21st century. All our conferences have been heavily centered on the idea of dialogue, under the motto "Dialogue of Civilizations for World Citizenship", and so in a way they constitute a practical extension of your over 1500 dialogues around the world.

Whenever we hold an international conference, we always try to select a location where the topic and issues are of particular relevance and concern in that place. The orientation of the conferences owes a lot to your credo: "Listen to the voices of people who are experiencing pain and stand by them".

Ikeda: I am grateful for your generous words. What I am trying to do is to carry on the legacy of my mentor in concrete and practical action to realize world peace. The Toda Institute was set up to be a center from which to mobilize the wisdom and resources of people at the grass roots level and to insist that the challenge for solutions to global issues must be part of a "common struggle of humankind".

When I founded the Institute and began thinking about its approach to research, I envisioned a new kind of policy research center resting on the support of many different kinds of people. I hoped to enlist academic and research organizations and NGOs from around the world to work together in building a network reaching through all nations, with the broad objectives of linking diverse groups and individuals engaged in peace-related activities and thereby helping to organize and enhance the "power of the people". I wanted to provide a way for people who have been working separately until now to join forces in their activities at a grass-roots level, so that they can play a bigger part in finding answers to the world's problems.

When you expressed your enthusiasm for and endorsement of these objectives upon becoming director of the Institute, I felt a new confidence that they would be pursued with determination. I am particularly interested in your ambitious plan to make full use of the latest information and communications technology to link people in peace-related activities throughout the world, making the Institute into what you have called a "fortress for peace".

Tehranian: During 1996 we at the Institute held a series of consultation meetings in Tokyo, Cambridge (USA), Honolulu, Hiroshima, York (UK), Tehran, Brisbane (Australia), and Toronto. We invited over two hundred peace and policy scholars from every continent to join our International Advisory Council. We have also established Internet links among the Council members that provide an email channel for exchange of opinions and continuing discussion and consultation. The Council is growing in size, encompassing a network of global citizens not just from academia, but also from government, business, and every level of civil society.

Concrete Proposals and Activities for Peace

Ikeda: It's admirable, what you have accomplished. Clearly research in peace is now at a major turning point. During the long years of the Cold War, peace research was aimed mainly at averting a catastrophic nuclear war and easing the strains of East-West confrontation. However, even before the fruits of that research could be put fully to use, the communist regimes in Eastern Europe were toppled by a series of revolutions and the Soviet Union began to break apart, bringing an end to the Cold War.

Of course this work is as important as ever as a source of warnings that can help prevent conflict from arising and confrontation from escalating. But the task of research in peace from now on will be to provide specific and workable alternatives for building peace in the world and a solid vision for the future. The new role of peace research is to lay the foundations for a new era.

Tehranian: I feel the same way. I mentioned this earlier, but back in 1996 when the Institute was launched and we on the staff were finalizing the statement of mission, we determined that it would be a "new kind of institute for a new kind of world". Our initial research program, which we call "Human Security and Global Governance" (HUGG), has the central aim of promoting peace initiatives and activities in nations and regions and proposing concrete policy options. Toda Institute is thus a growing network of peace and policy scholars spread throughout the world.

Ikeda: Peace research from now on will have the two trajectories of formulating concrete plans and charting a clear general direction for ideas and action; both are necessary. Josei Toda often emphasized the importance of concrete proposals and practical action in any efforts for peace. Even if they do not bear fruit immediately, he said, they will produce the glowing embers that stoke the worldwide fires of peace. Empty theories and polemics accomplish nothing, but concrete, practicable proposals can operate to change the status quo and then to be a shelter protecting all of humankind.

Following guidelines Mr. Toda instilled in me, I have tried, in the annual peace proposals that I have been presenting for twenty-five years and on appropriate anniversaries and on other occasions, to set out ideas for a constructive, beneficial course for the international community and specific approaches for specific problems, and I have continued activities intended to help realize new initiatives for peace.

Toda: An Inviolable Right to Live

Ikeda: Of all the projects I have ever been involved in, I have probably worked longest and hardest on the campaign to eliminate nuclear weapons. As you know, we in the SGI take the antinuclear manifesto delivered by Mr. Toda in September, 1957 as the starting point for our peace movement. One frequently quoted passage reads, "We, the citizens of the world, have an inviolable right to live. Anyone who tries to jeopardize this right is a devil incarnate, a fiend, a monster." Then came Mr. Toda's cry, "I want to tear out that evil at the roots of its deep, dark clutches."

It was a ferocious attack on the evil of weapons capable of obliterating human existence, and a fierce condemnation of the evil that haunts anyone responsible for producing nuclear weapons and anyone who would ever consider using them. The manifesto, issued just before his death, was Mr. Toda's final instructions to us younger members: our primary task, he said, was to rid the earth of these weapons of total destruction.

Including the circuit exhibitions "Nuclear Arms Threat to Our World" and "War and Peace", which were held in numerous cities throughout the world, Soka Gakkai has held or been involved in various peace-related projects. It has also been publishing a series of antiwar publications. Most recently the Youth Division supported the "Abolition 2000" campaign for the abolition of nuclear weapons, and was able to get 13 million signatures on a petition.

Tehranian: I am fully aware of your own unceasing work and SGI's tenacious efforts toward a world without nuclear weapons and the pursuit of peace. In fact, those ideals are what first drew me to SGI and its mission, and they are, as you know, on the top of the Toda Institute's research agenda as we try to follow the example he gave.

In September, 1997 we held a major HUGG conference on the theme "Non-nuclear Prerequisites for Nuclear Abolition" in Taplow Court, Maidenhead, UK. About thirty world-renowned scholars of arms control gathered there for a very significant consideration of how to eliminate the curse of nuclear weapons. The inaugural address was given by Joseph Rotblat, Peace Nobel laureate and a founding father and president of Pugwash, a pioneer in the struggle against nuclear weapons. I came away from that conference with a stronger sense of how prescient the Toda manifesto had been and a renewed faith in the necessity and urgency of our project. Mr. Toda's cry of anguish continues to echo in the minds and hearts of millions of world citizens.

Ikeda: The other aspect, of course, is the end of the Cold War. Now that it is part of history and the danger of all-out nuclear war has retreated, a certain sense of relief has settled in the international community. Public concern about nuclear weapons has tended to fade somewhat. As was demonstrated in no uncertain terms in the nuclear tests carried out by India in 1998, rapidly followed by Pakistan's tests, more and more nations are eager to have a nuclear capability. We are seeing a sort of domino effect, and this is going to lead to further nuclear proliferation. If we let it go on and do nothing, the human race is going to become trapped with no way out of the predicament.

Most unfortunate, the nuclear nations refuse to change their position that nuclear weapons are necessary to guarantee their security. They persist in holding firm to the presumed deterrent effect of nuclear weapons. What is it going to take to convince nations which already have a nuclear capability, and will not even consider talking about abolition, to change their policy? There are organizations that can play a valuable role here: they are the NGOs, in addition to other popular movements. Apparently the subject of NGOs and their importance was discussed at the HUGG conference in England, also.

Tehranian: That is right. The dangers of a nuclear war were one of the main issues brought up by David Krieger, president of the

Nuclear Age Peace Foundation, in his report, whose title was "From Arms Control to Abolition—Global Action Toward a Nuclear-Free World". During a brief intermission in his talk Krieger remarked to me that we really need much stronger pressure from international opinion if we ever, realistically, hope finally to get rid of nuclear weapons. "The sort of approach SGI is taking is going to become more and more important from now on", he said.

I, too, believe that people have the power to destroy the illusions of both nuclear possessors and hopefuls. I will never forget the power of Professor Rotblat's words in his keynote address at the Taplow Court conference:

"Even in our most pessimistic scenarios, we could not imagine that human society would be so unthinking as to accumulate this obscenely huge number of weapons for which we could see no purpose whatsoever. And yet, it turns out that human society was that unreflective."

It takes no more than basic human feeling and sensitivity to see the obscenity and insanity in the wish by any government to keep or to acquire nuclear weapons as a "necessary evil". And it will take serious and sustained courage by popular movements and communities everywhere to refuse to tolerate injustice. That courage is what we have come to expect from SGI's peace movement.

A Century of War—Never Again

Ikeda: I am glad you said that. I have never stopped believing that a world without nuclear weapons and a century without war could become reality only when people, not governments, became the driving force. Little by little as it expands its network of people wishing for peace, SGI has built a global solidarity based on the shared dream of ending all wars. Astronomical numbers of lives were lost in the maniacal wars of the twentieth century, leaving few of us completely untouched. In World War I an estimated 22 million, including civilians, died, and 60 million in World War II. It has been called a "century of war-deaths".

At enormous cost to humankind, we have finally learned that nothing is more tragic and cruel than war. Yet wars keep on coming as before, with no sign of letting up. We have become entangled in a cycle from which there is no way out without first shifting from a system of state-centered security to one of human-centered security. The stimulus and drive to accomplish that are going to come out of the popular, grass-roots peace movements.

Tehranian: As you say, security in international society has been primarily state-centric. Originating from the Peace of Westphalia in 1648, the traditional state system has primarily focused on inter-state security issues. Security studies have been consequently preoccupied with national and international security systems to the neglect of human security.

Of course it is true that some progress has been made in international security in the area of reductions and limitations on biological and chemical weapons. However, it is a lesson of history that when a country decides, in accord with its national policy, to go to war, the ones who are sacrificed are always the people. And not only war. Encroachments on human security in the form of famines, epidemics, domestic violence, civil wars, and environmental degradation have increased the need for reconsideration of the concept of security. There is now an emerging consensus to approach the problem more comprehensively.

In particular, reports by the United Nations Human Development Programme and the Commission on Global Governance have made significant contributions to formulating the new concepts of human security, and its realization has become the focus of attention throughout the international community.

Ikeda: I think human security demands broadening international law, extending its premises to foreground the interests of humanity, and supporting and strengthening the United Nations. International law was formed over the centuries-long tenure of the Westphalia system, developing as a set of rules that prioritized the adjustment of inter-state interests and privileged the traditional exclusive sovereignty of the state. So it is difficult to build consensus on the basis of the interests of humanity, or even if some agreement is reached, it is usually short-lived and hobbled by constraints that erode its practical effectiveness.

Tehranian: We can think of international relations as having developed historically through three broad stages, the first being the stage of "hard power", when the strong ruled the weak by coercion. In time and as states matured, hard power gave way to "hegemonic power", which, through the selective use of force and the power of persuasion, together with the application of some degree of international law, achieved a balance among states that preserved the international equilibrium. International law today takes shape within the parameters that defined those stages in previous historical eras.

But in an age of increasing globalization, crisis itself also assumes a global character, and the traditional responses of the past do not work anymore. There is a new challenge for us: to reformulate international law to give it a range and focus and purpose much wider than the narrow national interests dominating it now. We have entered a new era in which "soft power" sometimes works more effectively than hard or hegemonic power. Moral persuasions, cultural influences including food, music, art, and film, and litigation increasingly work more peacefully and effectively.

Making the United Nations a "Human Assemblage"

Ikeda: Turning to the United Nations, the fact is that it has been unable to break out of the constraints of the traditional framework of an assemblage of states, and it has not adequately fulfilled the purposes for which it was founded. But as you pointed out, "Today, for better or worse, the UN is the only organization to embody the unity of the world" (*Seikyo Shimbun*, December 25, 1993). We must give full support to the United Nations as it is now, but at the same time it is important that we try to turn it into an assembly that works for all the people on our planet.

When Secretary-General Boutros Boutros-Ghali and I met in the Fall of 1994, during our conversation I remarked that even though many people have had maximum expectations from the United Nations, it has in fact received only minimum support and assistance. For some time you, Professor Tehranian, have been urging the creation of a "People's Assembly" that can function creatively as a coordinating force. This is a very good idea. Now, when almost every nation is a member, I think the timing is good to pool know-how from around the world and seriously consider how the UN can be reformed to function as an "assemblage of humankind", a human agency.

Tehranian: I am glad that you are raising this question, because the Toda Institute is collaborating with La Trobe University (Australia) and Focus on Global South of Chulalongkorn University (Thailand) on what we affectionately call the "HUGG-UN" project. This is part of our HUGG project focusing on the possibilities for United Nations reform. Discussions with a group of experienced, eminent people are going on now. These have resulted in a series of proposals to democratize global governance at the UN and beyond. Two books on the topic have already been published.

My own personal view is that in order to make it responsive to the people's problems, we must democratize the UN structure, organization, and methods of operation as much as possible. Specifically, some good moves might be to reform the Security Council and the addition of a new organ to the UN General Assembly. Regarding the Security Council, first, the veto power of the five permanent members should be gradually diminished and eventually abolished. Second, the Security Council should be enlarged, and third, the principle of unanimity, with no veto power granted to anyone, should prevail in cases of resolutions calling for UN military intervention.

As for the General Assembly, a new, additional organization is needed to represent the people of the world independently of their states. The two assemblies could be called the States Assembly and the People's Assembly, with members of the latter elected on a representative basis such as that employed in the election of the European parliament.

Ikeda: Those are solid, valuable ideas. The People's Assembly in particular is something Johan Galtung, the peace scholar, and I agreed must be seriously considered. Nothing like this is going to happen overnight, of course, but it can be a practical objective, and when we remember that the UN Charter begins with the phrase, "We, the peoples of the United Nations", we have to remember the importance of sustained efforts to let the voices of people be heard. Until now, all we could see in the United Nations were the faces of nations. The UN should be reformed in the spirit of its founding to let the human faces—faces of people from all walks of life—become visible and their voices be heard in its operations and organization.

A Bigger Role for Non-state Actors

Tehranian: I think we can assume that the age of hegemonic power, with the system of nation-states as its organizing principle, has pretty much run out of steam. My views are close to those of Vaclav Havel, president of the Czech Republic, who describes our current situation as follows:

I think there are good reasons for suggesting that the modern age has ended. Today, many things indicate that we are going through a transitional period, when it seems that something is on the way out and something else is painfully being born. It is as if something were crumbling, decaying and exhausting itself, while something else, still indistinct, were arising from the rubble.

A truly evocative image. We cannot yet see the new infant, but it is there with throbbing heartbeats and birth pangs. We can also identify some of the new trends in the symbolism. In the post-Cold War era, non-state actors have assumed increasing momentum and power.

Ikeda: Recent activities of NGOs deserve special mention here. So far NGOs have made remarkable contributions in the areas of environment, human rights, and humanitarian projects, but recently in the area of arms reduction, too—until now the prerogative of national governments—they have had a considerable impact.

In July, 1996 the International Court of Justice issued the opinion that the threat to use or the use of nuclear arms in general violates international law, especially humanitarian law pertaining to violent conflict. What makes this opinion significant is that the real influence behind it was an NGO campaign formed around the World Court project. Then in September, 1997 a treaty to ban landmines was adopted. This was the result of activities by the International Campaign to Ban Landmines (ICBL) and other NGOs that moved a great many countries to sign the treaty at that time.

Tehranian: Both were epoch-making achievements showing the new power of non-state actors. In part because of the decline of superpower rivalries, such non-state actors have each achieved greater freedom in their own respective arenas of action. Besides NGOs, the non-state actors include transnational corporations (TNCs), transnational media organizations (TMCs) and others. It can be said that today, the world economy is basically run by the top five hundred or so major TNCs. The problem is that the TNCs are largely beyond government regulation or democratic control wherever they happen to be operating.

This economic activity is carried out mostly with the cooperation of agencies like the World Bank, the International Monetary Fund (IMF), and the World Trade Organization (WTO), together presiding over the long-range strategies of world economic development, foreign exchange stability, and the international division of labor and trade.

Ikeda: Certainly there are some among the TNCs that are capitalized and organized on a scale comparable to states. Their actions can shake the entire international community—we have seen that happen more than once. Given that these organizations have such a potent impact in the international economy, clearly a gap is going to open between those who make the rules of economic behavior and those who follow them.

Tehranian: Right. When a small or medium state dares to go against the policies of superpowers, TNCs, or intergovernmental organizations (IGOs), it can be punished through embargoes, trade sanctions, and denial of access to sources of world capital. That is why Toda Institute and its collaborators have proposed the creation of another consultative assembly within UN to be called "NGO Assembly", including business, civil society, and academic representatives.

Media: Who Are the Cheerleaders?

Tehranian: The ones who act mainly as the monitors and cheer-leaders in the process are the TMCs. News programs monitor world events but also construct the realities to which we respond. This is in part what you have called "soft power". But soft power can take so many different forms, positive as well as negative.

Ikeda: What do you mean?

Tehranian: So long as the major sources and channels of world news are Anglo-American, as they indeed have been for the past century or so, the realities constructed for mass audiences will continue to be one-dimensional. But TMCs are also channels for global advertising, a medium that promotes and legitimates consumerism. That is another form of soft power shaping the world today. Along the way, international travel, cultural trade, and the Internet also provide channels for exchange leading to cultural transmissions. While MacDonald's, Michael Jackson, Madonna, and CNN have penetrated the world markets, Japanese sushi, sashimi, and Kurosawa's films have also won the hearts of many people around the world.

Ikeda: That is true. In the case of news, because of the radical changes in communications technology, news from anywhere can be gotten live, as it happens, but as you said, today the news is largely transmitted through Anglo-American channels and so it takes that perspective. In volume of information, the greater part is delivered one-way from Anglo-American sources, hence not enough news from other areas goes the other way.

Still, development of the media and the Internet has made access to information wider and easier than it has ever been, and that can be seen as contributing to healthy democratic growth. Furthermore, through the media more people learn about conditions caused by environmental disasters, for instance, and the situation of refugees in far-flung corners of the globe, and that provides the opportunity to start and expand campaigns to do something about such problems.

New Possibilities for the Media and Democracy

Tehranian: Soft power itself is value-neutral. It can be employed for good or evil. It can elevate life or cheapen it. It can promote inter-national understanding or exacerbate cultural stereotypes through negative portrayals of certain ethnic, racial, religious, or national groups. Of course rapidly expanding global communication provides hope for achieving greater long-term understanding among nations and cultures, but the cluttering of the channels by episodic news of violence without any serious analysis of its root causes and possible remedies is leading to systematic distortions in communi-cation and knowledge. Most news is framed in narrow partisan and nationalist terms. But a global marketplace and society demand global norms, citizenship, and journalism.

Ikeda: Reporting should become more responsible, free from any underlying bias toward certain interests or complicity in a particular agenda. That means a new ethics for journalism that lifts it away from any kind of national or partisan slant.

Tehranian: The new ethics would have important implications for the practice of internationalism and for peacemaking, also. It calls for global journalism as an exercise in global citizenship. To me, the real challenge for the media is to employ soft power for international peace and understanding. Take the anti-landmine campaigne, which you mentioned earlier, and think what they have done. It is a remarkable example of the consummate skill with which an effective soft power campaign can be carried out. For six years, using the Internet and the World Wide Web as a means of disseminating information and communication, they mobilized more than one thousand NGOs, millions of world citizens to engage in an informed and effective campaign. They succeeded in convincing well over a hundred countries to sign the treaty banning landmines, and it went into effect in March, 1999. It is a phenomenon well worth emulating. Even so, the United States, Russia and China, all with huge arsenals of landmines, have refused so far to sign.

Ikeda: There has to be a way to stir up international feeling strong enough to convince these countries. All countries should be party to the treaty. A lot of people were very pessimistic about the treaty at first. In a way, its success speaks volumes about the merits of trying the "Ottowa process"—pushing a treaty through with the support only of those countries initially willing to sign. As you noted, the International Campaign to Ban Landmines (ICBL) turned out to be a monumentally successful landmark in world history.

The fact that the treaty, which has no loopholes and makes no exceptions, did not flounder was due partly to the strategy of making public the list of countries that opposed it and keeping the pressure on in other ways. Second, toward governments that initially demurred on grounds of "national defense", the ICBL was extremely tenacious in persuading them to rethink their position and finally come through.

When the 1997 Nobel peace prize award to the ICBL was announced in October, 1997, the committee cited the amazing achievements of the campaign, saying that it provides an example for similar campaigns in the future to mobilize international efforts toward arms reduction and peace. That statement was an expression of hope that people can become a determined, self-motivating force to push through a campaign for arms reduction.

Tehranian: By putting the Internet and communications technology to good use, the ICBL was a first attempt to break the barriers of the old ways of decision making. The erosion of democracy through a campaign financing system that puts the politicians at the service of donors, including arms manufacturers, rather than citizens, can thus be partially corrected by a mobilized civil society. But this would take active and informed citizens. The Internet provides a new democratic sphere of public discourse in which citizens can be globally informed, empowered, educated, and mobilized on specific issues. The case of landmines illustrates how the new cyber-democracy can work effectively through education and mobilization. All it takes is a compassionate citizen with a computer, a modem, and an Internet server.

Ikeda: The newest technologies have the power both to make our world a better place and to do serious harm. We have to be very aware of how these technologies work and all the ways in which they can be used, and then we can fully employ them to be of value to people. I think we have to keep that basic attitude toward technology.

Buddhist teaching stresses the need for wisdom to improve life. The positive aspects of the Internet and other elements in the "information revolution" include their nonexclusivity, as you pointed out. Now, knowledge and information are widely available, not just the preserve of one sector or group of people. They can be shared democratically by anyone who wishes to gain access.

What will become more important, moreover, is not just knowledge and information, *per se*, but the wisdom and discipline to use them well. To gain that wisdom, there is no better way than the meeting of hearts and minds through dialogue among our fellow human beings. In a true meeting of minds, there never arises the problem of one-way flow of knowledge or floods of meaningless information. From the counterpoint of voices and hearts reaching to connect through the ever-moving drama of dialogue spring new, lively ideas and fresh perceptions.

Tehranian: May I mention two caveats? First, Internet is not universally accessible—a problem that has come be known as the Digital Divide. Although it has rapidly expanded from zero to 500 million people within two decades, its growth has been primarily limited to high income countries and people (e.g. over 50 percent of Internet access is concentrated in the United States). Second, although we have focused primarily on macro-problems so far, peace can be most effectively achieved in the domain of micro-problems. As you say, dialogue is the key in both domains. However, dialogical communication can be obtained more effectively in face-to-face encounters and in small circles than in distantiated and mediated communication with large numbers. That is why, along with E.F. Schumacher, I believe "small is beautiful". We can achieve intimacy, understanding, and compassion more effectively in small numbers, within the family, friendship, and faith circles. That is why I highly value the role of such voluntary associations as SGI. At the level of modern states and corporations, abstraction, impersonality, greed, and aggression tend to predominate.

Humanitarian Competition—An Appeal to the Angels, Not the Demons, of Our Spirits

Ikeda: I appreciate your comments about SGI. Going back to the NGO activities, it seems to me that Toda's idea of global transnationalism, or what we call global citizenship has come into its own in our era. He always said, "It is wrong that any people be sacrificed, whoever they may be. We must go out and wipe the word 'misery' from the face of the earth." The source of that idea is Makiguchi's concept of "humane competition", representing an ideal of shared happiness and well being in the life of all people.

In 1903 Makiguchi's *A Geography of Human Life* was published. The plea he made in that book is that humankind should be beyond military competition, political competition, and economic competition. He said it is time that we shifted to humanitarian competition. He went on to say: It should be understood that "humanitarian approach" does not imply that there is a specific method which can be designated as such. Rather, it is an effort to plan and conduct whatever strategies, whether political, military, or economic, in a more humanitarian way. The important thing is the setting of a goal of well-being and protection of all people, including oneself but not at the increase of self interest alone. In other words, the aim is the betterment of others and in doing so, one chooses ways that will yield personal benefit as well as benefit to others. It is a conscious effort to create a more harmonious community life, and it will take considerable time for us to achieve.

Tehranian: It is really amazing to think that this supremely current and articulate vision of mutually supportive human community should have been written one hundred years ago. It directly addresses a most urgent task we have now, which is to move from confrontation to cooperation. In the Hobbesian view of the state of nature, the world is dominated by a war of all against all, where life is "solitary, poor, nasty, brutish, and short". The Hobbesian view of human security has been a zero-sum game; more security for one state spells less security for all the others.

Ikeda: What the international community should be trying to build, then, is a world where everyone is a winner, not a world that produces losers. In one of my peace proposals, I talked about one example of what I mean, which is the vision and challenge President Mandela of South Africa set for his nation: to build a "rainbow nation" where there is no discrimination on the basis of skin color.

Tehranian: I read that proposal and found it very thought provoking. The Mandelian view of human security begins with cooperation rather than competition as its premise. It envisions a modern democratic, multiracial society in which the security and welfare of each is the precondition for the security and welfare of all. This cooperative concept of security presumes a win-win game. Instead of the Hobbesian dark pessimism, Mandela starts with the optimistic assumption of potential good within each human being. This concept appeals to the angels rather than the demons of our spirits.

Ikeda: He seems to say that we cannot go on without a spiritual revolution taking place within each one of us. For a society of winners, we need more than mental conviction. It is going to take a radical change deep within our souls.

Professor Rotblat once talked with me about how war has the power to turn humans into bestial creatures. Once war breaks out, there are scientists who, ordinarily clear and firm in distinguishing good and bad, suddenly lose their ability to judge correctly. Those who condemned barbarity in peacetime find themselves doing barbarous acts in times of war. That, he said, is the madness of war.

Tehranian: Such madness, not just in war, has brought so much tragedy of all kinds to the human race. I think of all the pain, and then realize how people keep making the same mistakes over and over again. I cannot help feeling that the real heart of the problem may lie in something very deep, perhaps best called human karma.

Ikeda: The Buddhist concept of "ten worlds" sets out ten potential conditions of life inherent in every individual human life. The life condition of a person caught up in war is in the lower conditions of "hell" (dominated by powerlessness), "hunger" (dominated by greed), "animality" (foolish unreason), and "anger" (selfish ego). The first three together are called the "three evil paths", and all four are collectively called the "four evil paths". In general, this condition is dominated by naked instinct and greed; the person is governed totally by reactions to external influences. The thoughts and behavior of people in such a condition are inescapably stupid, foolish, and savage.

In the Buddhist view, this state is to be expected. We might achieve a superficial, externally-generated peace, but even if we do, it will be a fragile thing that will crumble at the slightest disturbance. It may be more circuitous, but the foundation for real, unbreakable peace is to build peace in the hearts of people, each individual. In other words, to cultivate personal, inner peace in all of us.

What we in the SGI have been doing is trying to stimulate this kind of "human revolution" in people all over the world, trying to help them build their own inner peace. I will always have faith that humanity can extricate itself from the conflicts and violence imposed by the vicissitudes of fate when the internal change in human lives, coming like wave upon wave on the shore, turns into a swelling tumult of people with the wisdom of inner peace.

Tehranian: You have wisely raised the question of outer and inner peace. A Persian poet expressed it well when he said: How can an entity without life give life to other living entities? How can a person without inner peace extend peace to others? That seems to me to be an impossible task. The outer world is a very complex and conflict-ridden place and is becoming more so. None of us can claim to be able to establish peace in this world once and for all, but we can all make a contribution. Where shall we start? Nowhere is more amenable to our influence than our own selves.

The Sufis consider mastering the unbridled self (*nafs-i-ammareh*) as the most challenging task in life. A Sufi precept teaches us that the unbridled self is our greatest enemy. It constantly tempts us toward self-righteousness, anger, greed, hatred, and aggression.

Ikeda: Absolutely. One of the essential points in Buddhist teaching is the necessity to develop self-discipline and self-restraint.

Tehranian: The Sufis also recognize another self within each of us ready to be awakened by a little education, discipline, and compassion. This divine self craves love, charity, and transcendence, and it can ultimately dissolve selfhood in a higher state of being in union with God. Whichever way we look at it, overcoming the dualism between the self and others is the key to an enlightened and peaceful life.

As long as we continue considering our interests as distinct and in opposition to others, we will be generating conflict. The moment we discover ourselves as part of a larger design of being, interdependent with all other life forms, we will be seeking ways to resolve conflicts, which are the inevitable part of our apparently separate physical existence.

Ikeda: That idea has much in common with the Buddhist concept of *engi* (dependent origination), the idea that basically nothing arises without ties to everything else. So in the human world or in the natural world, there is not a single phenomenon that comes into being or exists on its own, independent from everything else. All things are interrelated and interdependent, together forming the great cosmos and constantly changing.

To live, to "discover ourselves as part of a larger design of being", and to look on life, the most universal dimension of being, with the profound gaze of the poet is itself to have sympathy with all the infinitude of diversity. That is what I hope all people will experience. The sympathy that is born out of the depths of life, encompassing equality and dignity, is what prevails in the core of our being, the wellspring of a world of human harmony.

Tehranian: We may talk about living together, but a superficial tolerance that simply accepts the existence of others is not enough.

Ikeda: Yes. We need to find what it is that, beyond the level of mental attitudes, originates in a sense of the totality surging up from the depths of life, a sense of the cosmos. The Buddhist expression *esho-funi* (oneness of life and its environment) teaches us that the essential dynamic of life and the environment are two and at the same time not two, always together. The way humans, as subject, live, the conditions of their lives, exerts a strong influence on the environment. Without inner peace, therefore, it is very difficult to achieve external peace.

But there is also some danger that in this agitated world, peace in our hearts alone will get us little more than empty, abstract theories. The pursuit of peace and accord in our world has to be joined with practical action. With concrete, viable strategies in place, "peace" will begin to take shape as a practical reality and settle into society. Through the struggle, the inner peace of all individuals will be tempered and refined into something that will never break. I have firm faith that this dynamic antiphon between the quest for inner peace and practical action will have the power eventually to move an era.

Tehranian: I would identify your antiphony as natural spirituality and practical wisdom, as different from asceticism (renunciation of the world) or self-indulgence. In Christianity, the latter are known as the cardinal sins of pride and sensuality.

CHAPTER 10

A Century of Peace?

Ikeda: Developing a sense of world citizenship and the mission of young people will be very important in the coming century. Let me turn back for a while and take a look at the 20th century, a time we have all lived through and which forms the backdrop to the future.

Isaiah Berlin, the British historian and writer, has said words to the effect that, "No other century can be compared to the twentieth century in its savagery, for the merciless slaughter people inflicted on each other time and again. That is the disheartening realization we must live with now". Berlin's words are hardly necessary to remind us that in frequency, scale, and level of brutality, the 20th century carried human tragedy to extremes that have no comparison in any other period of history.

Tehranian: It is certainly true that the 20th century has been the bloodiest in all known human history. From the first and second world wars to Hitler's holocaust, Pol Pot's massacres, and all the postwar bloody conflicts in Korea, Vietnam, the Persian Gulf, and more—leaving no breathing space, they caused the death and destruction of millions of people. Over 170 million people were killed by governments in official acts of genocide such as the Holocaust.

Since 1900, about 250 new international and civil wars have been waged in which over 100 million soldiers and another 100 million civilians have died. Counting only military casualties, the 18th century had a casualty rate of 50 per million population per year as compared to 60 per million during the 19th century and over 460 per million for the 20th century.

Can we turn the 21st century into a century of peaceful life? As we continue to make "progress" in the hit/kill ratio of weapons, the new century might be even bloodier. Many perplexing problems remain unsolved, hindering the realization of global peace.

Ikeda: The unproductive confrontation of ideologies seems finally to have subsided, but divisive energies continue to roil to the surface in tragic explosions throughout the world. As soon as the idea of ethnicity was given an independent existence separated from reality, it became sacrosanct, and it was made the rationale for the carnage in the former Yugoslavia, in Africa, most notoriously Rwanda, and elsewhere. Berlin's "disheartening realization" of thirty years ago by no means belongs only to the past.

Tehranian: That is true. If we add structural violence, which goes on unnoticeably in the slow death of millions suffering from famine, malnutrition, epidemics, or homelessness, the 20th century could legitimately be called a century of death by design. Unlike other centuries, in the 20th century, murder of millions was carefully designed by the most advanced scientific methods and weapons of mass destruction.

In contrast to these mass murders, the 20th century has been also a century of spectacular achievements in science and technology outpacing human progress in intellectual and spiritual under-standing. As the two recent wars in the Persian Gulf (1980–88, 1990–91) demonstrated, we have improved our technologies and engineering of death well beyond our moral imagination.

Ikeda: The tendencies of such an era will change only when there is a fundamental change in values. I think the first step has to begin with a clear-headed examination of the history behind the tragedies that have occurred so that we can learn something from them.

Tehranian: In that regard, we may identify at least three kinds of cultural learning: additive, regenerative, and transformative. Additive learning is typical of scientific and technological learning in which knowledge tends to be accumulative and accelerating. Regenerative learning is the moral knowledge that is passed on from one generation to another; it often has to be relearned through the pains and sufferings of each new generation. That is why wars recur and each generation makes some of the same mistakes of the previous ones.

Ikeda: You are saying that regenerative learning cannot be accumulated. So each generation has to experience their own pain and agony, and through that, rediscover the core values of their own culture and society. Then they have to adjust and change those values to fit the current times and environment. Is that what you mean?

Tehranian: Yes, that's right. And in contrast, transformative learning is a type of moral and spiritual knowledge that comes about sluggishly through the inspirations of great spiritual leaders who take giant steps forward by integrating the collective learning of all past generations. Such great moral breakthroughs are the equivalent of big technological breakthroughs in history. They reverberate in the sinews of society for centuries to come until they are finally institutionalized. Such are the teachings of our great masters from Zoroaster to Buddha, Confucius, Lao-tze, Abraham, Moses, Jesus, Mohammed, Nichiren, and Gandhi.

Crisis of Humanity and the Human Spirit—A Pivotal Age

Ikeda: It is significant that so many great leaders appeared during the centuries between 800 B.C. and 200 B.C., a "pivotal age" as Karl Jaspers called it. As you pointed out, that time saw the birth of Shakyamuni and the founding of Upanishad philosophy in India, and the appearance of Confucius, Lao-tze, and other great thinkers in China. In Persia Zoroaster preached the doctrine of struggle between good and evil, while Elijah, Isaiah, the second Isaiah, and the other great Hebrew prophets arose in Palestine.

Tehranian: That was also a golden age of magnificent achievements in Greece—Homer and the two ageless epics he created; Heraclitus, Socrates, Plato, Aristotle, and the other great philosophers; Archimedes and the many others who changed the world of science, mathematics, architecture.

Ikeda: In *Vom Ursprung und Ziel der Geschichte* (1949) [The Origin and Goal of History] by Karl Jaspers, the author says that, "Until today mankind has lived by what happened during the Axial Period, by what was thought and created during that period". There must be some reason that so many spiritual giants happened to live and work around the same period. Why is it that in the span of a few centuries, many of the greatest thinkers who have ever lived paraded into the world, one after another? Jaspers argues that they arose at a time when people were pressured to develop a consciousness of their identity as a whole and of the boundaries of that existence. Out of the spiritual transformation that accompanied the upheavals of the times, ideas and religions were born that reverberated far into the ages that followed.

Yet now the influence of that first "Axial Period" is fading, and our era is fast sinking into unguided confusion. I have become convinced that humankind has to make a whole new start. It is time for another deep spiritual transformation, which will come about as we seek to erect a new, solid foundation on which to build a global society of human coexistence.

Tehranian: Indeed, that is one of the urgent tasks we have now.

Ikeda: I find the insights of Dr. Sissela Bok of Brandeis University to be extremely relevant to the question of how we can find a way to make a new start. She points out that all people can share the same values. Her words go something like this: "There is no need to search for new values. What is crucial rather, is to critically reexamine the values that already exist." She goes on to say, "And I cannot overemphasize the point that values are of use only when they are made to work in real life". I think it would be very worthwhile to examine ideologies and philosophies in terms of their universality and their realism, the qualities Bok sees as most important.

Tehranian: Extremely worthwhile and very challenging. Before I respond, let me first contextualize my position by outlining the current philosophic tendencies. At one extreme, we have the modernists or secular humanists arguing that to further progress, the principles of modern science and technology provide a necessary and sufficient basis for a global ethics of human rights and democratic participation. From this point of view, religious worldviews are at best inconsequential or at worst an obstacle to human progress.

At the other extreme, we have the postmodernists negating the validity of any metanarrative, whether religious or secular. From their point of view, all metanarratives or teleological philosophies of history are actually or potentially hegemonic projects aiming, consciously or unconsciously, at domination or exploitation.

Ikeda: It seems to me that the postmodernists include a lot of very skeptical souls who are out to demystify or to search out fabrications in traditional religions and ideologies.

Tehranian: Yes. The postmodernists are radical sceptics engaged in a strategy of deconstruction and demystification of the ideological pretenses of both religious and secular persuaders.

Third, we have a complex variety of religious and secular worldviews trying to adapt their own traditions of civility in order to develop an ethics commensurate with the increasing complexities of our world. Among them we can find fundamentalists as well as mystics, totalitarians as well as liberals, and idealists as well as pragmatists.

I consider myself a seeker who, like Gandhi, likes to experiment with truth without claiming to have found it. I believe that the moment you claim to have found the truth, you have lost it because that stops you from seeking further for knowledge and wisdom, which itself requires you to negotiate with other people in the common search for truth. In my mind, that would be tantamount to renouncing dialogue. My truth is therefore the search for truth through dialogue.

Ikeda: I can understand that very well. Gandhi believed that truth is God, rather than God is truth, and he rejected any kind of sectarianism. Speaking about truth, he said, "I am devoted to none but Truth and I owe no discipline to anybody but Truth." And, "It is my firm faith … that we can conquer the whole world by truth and love".

Gandhi also spoke of truth as "that which you believe to be true at this moment," "deposited in every human heart", and the realization of "oneself and one's destiny". His approach to truth was in many ways very practical even while it was deeply internal. That is why he could say, "What is possible for one person is possible for everyone".

Tehranian: I agree. At the very core of Gandhi's practice of nonviolence (*ahimsa*) and his *satyagraha* movement was his belief in the essential goodness of human nature and the dialogue that appeals to that goodness. That is why he did not discriminate against his foes, but treated them as humans. He asked of his friends and foes that they follow the same path and look within themselves to discover the right path.

Many British colonialists could not help being profoundly affected by the courage and humility of this frail and steely man. He once noted that the commander of the British forces in India, who had put him in jail, was suffering from holes in his boots. In prison, Gandhi took the pains to make a new pair of boots for the British general and sent it to him as a gift with his best wishes. For the rest of his life, the general proudly displayed those boots in his office as a symbol of the friendship between India and Britain. That is the kind of religious and humanist spirit that we need to propagate around the world.

Ikeda: As I understand it, in Gandhi's view religion is not a matter of sects, but is concerned with faith in a moral order governing the universe. Religion can change us as individuals by uniting us with the truth that resides within and thereby purify us; that aspect of humanity is eternal, he said. What our society today needs is exactly such an open and accepting spirituality and religiosity.

Open and Accessible Religion

Tehranian: As you suggest, I also think the universal religious foundations of Gandhi's faith have given it a perennial relevance, regardless of time and space. That is why the philosophy of nonviolence and its methods have been adopted in a variety of places and situations during this century. In the United States' civil rights movement, in the South African struggle against apartheid, in the eastern European overthrow of communist dictatorships, even in Palestine and Ireland, the methods have been effectively tried and met with total or partial success. The key to this success is, of course, a particular view of religion not as a path for personal salvation alone but also for social action on behalf of peace and justice.

Ikeda: What you are saying, then, is that Gandhi saw religion as being more than a force that affects only our internal, personal lives. Gandhi's religion reaches more deeply into the life of society, governing the way people conduct themselves in the world. This way of thinking reminds me of the Mahayana idea that religion is the source of all human activity.

Tehranian: The operative concept is, of course, the connection between religion and action, namely nonviolence. In Hinduism and Buddhism, *ahimsa* or the principle of noninjury to living beings is a central tenet. The Koran's chapters each begin with the phrase, "In the name of God, the Compassionate and the Merciful". In Islam, *jihad* has been sometimes interpreted as Holy War. But a careful analysis of the term and its practice by Prophet Muhammad shows that taking to arms has been allowed in Islam only in self-defense. That is called external *jihad*. Internal *jihad* is considered far more difficult and challenging. It consists of purifying the soul of its impurities—greed, aggression, and evil. In Sufism this is called *jihad-i-akbar* or the Great Jihad.

Ikeda: Christian teaching also emphasizes nonviolence, as you have pointed out. Didn't Jesus say, "Those who live by the sword shall die by the sword"?

Tehranian: Yes. That was Jesus' admonition to the apostle Peter. In all great religions, therefore, violence is condemned while love, compassion, and charity are condoned. Also in all great religious traditions, we can point to times and circumstances in which bigotry and violence have been sanctioned on religious grounds. We are thus faced with the paradox of noble doctrines and not-so-noble practitioners. For this reason, modern secular humanism in its varieties of forms (Marxism, existentialism, and postmodernism) has attempted to restore to human freedom what it considers some religious traditions have taken away. While Marxism replaces historical necessity for divine determinism, existentialism and postmodernism opt for a radical position on human freedom.

Ikeda: Jean-Paul Sartre, whose existentialist philosophy reveals the influence of Kierkegaard, talked about human freedom in ways that have become part of every thinking person's vocabulary.

Tehranian: In one of Sartre's most memorable pronouncements, humans are said to be "condemned to freedom". Going through the experience of World War II and writing in the bleak postwar period, Sartre envisioned a universe without meaning in which the individual must live a lonely but free and responsible life. In a universe where "God is dead", as Nietzsche proclaimed, humans are faced with the terrifying responsibility of not only choosing for themselves but also for all others.

As Sartre points out, in every choice we make we must consider its moral and practical implications, assuming always the consequences of our action's universal adoption by others.

Ikeda: And that offers people a good reason to maintain a kind of consideration for others.

Tehranian: Yes. If humanism is defined that way, it contains no necessary contradiction with the humanitarian religious traditions. As Soren Kierkegaard and Paul Tillich demonstrated, we can be religious rather than secular humanists or existentialists. As I understand them, that is the central meaning of Soka, or Mahayana, and Sufi traditions. Instead of relegating decisions to rigid religious dogma or to the superior wisdom of some spiritual leader, every believer is asked to make conscious moral decisions on his or her own authority and take the consequences. Every individual is thus assumed to have the potentiality to rise above his or her own petty self-interest to reach out for the universal good.

Ikeda: The basic spirit of Buddhism, as you said, is to abide by the Law, not by human dictates. The Law embraces the eternal, invariable rules governing the universe and the inner discipline that springs from human life. There is, therefore, no contradiction with science or ethics. Rather, the Law becomes the force motivating activity and growth among people, within the lives we lead, and on into society.

Tehranian: The idea of *Tariqa*, the Way, which is central to Sufism, also stresses the spirit of the Law. Sufism emphasizes the inner life of the spirit; the human obligation to pursue the good and social service over pure dogma; and the quest for life lived according to the Way over the pursuit of fidelity to the forms of religious duty.

Ikeda: Practice is the important thing, how an individual expresses spiritual truths in the way she or he lives. To live according to the Way means to live by the Law following truth and reason. You have to decide to live autonomously, empowered by inner motivation rather than guided by external rules or pressures. That kind of life takes exceedingly strong self-discipline. But the only way religions can combat the pernicious influences of fanaticism, exclusivity, authoritarianism, rigid dogmatism, and so forth is by the efforts of the faithful to foster such self-discipline and practice it in their lives. I am also convinced that this is the way to overcome what you called the paradox of "noble doctrine and not-so-noble practitioners".

Soka Gakkai's first president, Tsunesaburo Makiguchi, spent his life standing up against authoritarian, oppressive religious views and trying to bring religion back to the people. Firm in his beliefs, until the day he died in prison he fought against the powers that shamelessly sought to use people in the name of religion. We, his successors, have inherited that spirit, and it continues to inspire us to keep fighting.

Tehranian: I have always found the struggles of the past presidents of Soka Gakkai to be a source of great inspiration. Reversing the priority, from "people to serve religion" to "religion for the sake of people", was an important achievement.

Ikeda: That brings us to the key issue here, which is how the individual can manifest the potential capacities intrinsic to a human life, "to rise above his or her petty self-interest to reach out for the universal good", to use your phrase. One of the Buddhist commentaries contains a beautiful passage: "When you bow toward the mirror, the image in the mirror bows toward you" (*Gosho*, p. 769). It is telling us that when you respect the life of another person, like the image in a mirror, you will realize the nobility of your own life.

In other words, you can change a self-centered life by "always respecting others as inseparable from yourself" (*jita funi no raihai*). That means looking at all of life and seeing it as not separate from yourself, but as something that embraces you and all other beings in a shared existence. The same commentary says, "Joy is when you share happiness with others" (*Gosho*, p. 761). If each person continues to practice that teaching, a new sense of values will begin to spread throughout society, and those values will restrain people from trying to build their own happiness first, at the expense of the happiness of others.

The distress we in the modern world experience seems to me to stem from our loss of a sense of what binds people together. Self-centered egotism, in all its many and sundry forms, is a kind of divisive energy that causes confrontations and disputes. We can see them erupting all over the world.

Overcoming Ethnic Conflict

Ikeda: One of the biggest unsolved problems the new century inherits from the old is the increasingly serious friction arising around what people think of as ethnic groups. After a long period of colonial rule and other forms of domination, which created manifold suffering and sacrifice, the idea of cultural relativism has finally begun to take root as an affirmation of a kind of equality.

The trouble is, although the term cultural relativism would appear to be value-free, it is precisely such consciousness-raising self-affirmation that can become a source of constant instability for an ethnic group by weakening the motivation to make positive efforts toward stable, healthy communities. The concept actually involves the danger of encouraging people to embrace nationalism or ethnocentrism at any moment, which can then lead to social disruption and bare oppression. When your neighbor of today becomes your enemy tomorrow, that is tragedy. And that is what has torn apart the people of Rwanda, the former Yugoslavia, and elsewhere.

Tehranian: Historically, societies have dealt with the problem of ethnic, religious, and cultural diversity in many different ways. History is replete with cultural policies that have tried to mold identities to suit the reasons of the state. From the most inhumane to the most humane, such policies have ranged from extermination to expulsion, segregation, assimilation, amalgamation, and integration. The cruelest strategy has been to exterminate those who are not like us. Policies of extermination have been pursued in the cases of Jews in Hitler's Germany, and Muslims in Bosnia.

The diversity in our cultures and societies is a source of great enrichment of the human experience, but at the same time each society and culture has the potential to destroy the bonds among people. By strengthening the cultural tendencies toward peace, we may build societies that reward peace and discourage violence.

Ikeda: To me, an intrinsic aspect of culture is that it makes human life richer, more satisfying, but used in the sense of "a culture", the same word can also become simply another term describing something to which a person "belongs". The problem with the latter is the possibility of "cultural absolutism" developing so as to justify exclusionist policies and behavior.

As soon as you start categorizing people according to race or ethnicity, the affective sense of belonging, of being part of the same humanity, is lost and your ability to empathize stops working.

Freud had a term for this condition buried within the psyche; he called it "narcissism in respect of minor differences". As long as such "minor differences" continue to matter, it remains very difficult to stop the vicious circle of endlessly mounting, diminishing, and recurring conflict. As is being unexpectedly borne out by events in the world today, Hobbes' idea of the legal state has been of no help at all in creating a "communitarian" world where people from every kind of background can enjoy freedom and well-being equally.

Tehranian: Indeed, Hobbes became convinced that life in the state of nature is a war of all against all, and in such a world, in order to safeguard peace and social order, we must have strong and centralized governments with dictatorial powers providing sanctions against this human tendency toward evil. The Hobbesian view of human security was thus a zero-sum game—more security for one spelled out less security for all the others. His solution to the dilemmas of competitive security was, therefore, to submit personal sovereignties in the state of nature to a Leviathan, a national

Sovereign who would provide security for all while demanding obedience to his laws.

This Hobbesian social contract was considered to be a *sine qua non* of all human security and welfare. But all the so-called just wars waged and violence legitimized under the system of modern sovereign states have clearly done nothing but make the problem worse. A new system is required, a democratic system that can block violent initiatives by those in power. Even more, human beings need to go through a major spiritual change if we can ever hope to move from a culture of war to a culture of peace.

Ikeda: There is a good chance that uniting ethnic and other groups will produce peace and well-being, but there is no chance at all if these groups are separated. Identity is a source of serious anxiety today. People are intense about wanting to belong to a defined group. For them, the lure of ethnicity can play on the emotions. I suspect, however, that the sense of ethnic belonging is something intentionally fostered, and that "ethnicity" is an artifice of modern history.

Rabindranath Tagore, the Indian poet, got it right in *The Religion of Man* (1931) when he talked about the substance of ethnicity. As I recall, he said that the great prophets of all eras experienced true freedom of the spirit because they were aware that the human spirit has a universal aspect. Even so, circumstances like geography isolated them, and certain ethnic groups developed increasingly self-centered ways of thinking.

Tehranian: The 20th century has been trampled upon by the divisive energies of such products of false consciousness as tribalism, ethnocentrism, and nationalism. Many wars broke out as people were dragged about by fictitious values and ideas. For all the combatants, the collision of territorial claims has been increasingly clothed in greater moral self-righteousness, exploiting the pull of ethnicity. The adversaries are playing to an ever-growing gallery of global audiences watching them on television screens. As the mass media dichotomize, dramatize, and demonize "them" against "us", reified images of the "Islamic terrorists", "satanic Americans", "cunning Japanese", "evil Chinese", and "uncivilized Africans" become frozen in the minds of mass audiences as justifications for the next cycle of violence.

Ikeda: Racial and ethnic stereotypes are insidious. Once fixed in the mind, they are exceedingly hard to erase. Too often they lie behind some otherwise unremarkable dispute that ignites a full-blown conflict. Tagore warns us about the danger brewing in racial and ethnic confrontations. The problem of race looming over us will eventually compel us to abandon the search for superficial measures, driving us to the point where we have no choice but to make mental adaptations. Otherwise, we will find ourselves immobilized, unable to act because racial differences will have produced so many seeds of conflict. Ultimately the racial issue will be the cause of our doom. More than half a century has passed since he sent out this warning. It is enough to make one despair to look back and realize that not only do the tragic follies of humans seem never to end, but today they have deepened to crisis proportions.

What World Citizenship Should Be

Tehranian: You have raised one of the most troubling problems of our times. It involves the question that all of us face as we struggle with the need to know "Who am I?" "To what or whom do I owe my loyalty?" We are all now faced with the choice to stay either narrow and parochial in our identities and loyalties or broaden our scope to embrace the rest of the world. Because of the forces of economic and cultural globalization, however, this is no longer a free choice. It is a choice being thrust upon us. In traditional societies where people were born, lived, and died in the same small village or town, we can assume that such a problem did not exist. People were certain of their identities, which were defined in terms of family, language, religion, and culture. With the rise of the modern world, physical, social, and psychic mobility has increased at an ever-accelerating rate. A majority of people nowadays no longer live in the place where they were born. Most other people are thoroughly exposed to other societies and cultures through travel, professional contacts, or the media.

Ikeda: All the conditions for the rise of the modern-day identity crisis.

Tehranian: At such times people have to renegotiate their identities in their new cultural and social encounters. If we wish to live in a more peaceful world, we have no other alternative but to accept that we all belong to a complex variety of communities, identities, and loyalties. We are all, in this sense, multicultural, and we need to negotiate with others and ourselves an identity and citizenship that is inclusive rather than exclusive. Beyond space and time we also belong to the world of the spirits. We'll be happier if we could transcend our own bounded self to partake in the cosmic self.

Ikeda: Almost a hundred years ago, Tsunesaburo Makiguchi published a book called *A Geography of Human Life*. In that work he argued that every individual needs three different types of self-consciousness. First, the person is aware of being "local", concerned about both home and neighboring communities. Second, the individual should have a sense of belonging to a nation. Third, that person should also see him/herself as cosmopolitan, a citizen of the world. In Makiguchi's vision, every one of us needs a foothold in both a "homeland" and in the world.

Our position must be sure enough to withstand pressure from wrongheaded national policies and confident enough to enable us to appreciate and understand others. It must be our base for living as good neighbors and good citizens, advocates of coexistence and shared prosperity, whether we are working locally or in international society. In effect, Makiguchi dreamed of a world where people had the breadth and height of vision to be able to look both ways at the same time—toward the world and toward home.

Tehranian: Makiguchi was extremely prescient in having foreseen the kind of global citizenship that is only now getting due recognition. It is important to remember that the individual has a choice of multiple identities, at the local, national, regional, and global levels.

Ikeda: You have made some important observations about what I think of as growing interdependence on every level, compelling the individual to develop a sense of self that goes beyond the parochial to relate to all humankind. But it may be counterproductive to try to rush everyone into becoming global citizens at once; too many will end up being like fragile, rootless grass without local or national identity.

The French philosopher Simone Weil wrote convincingly about the need for "roots" in life. If, indeed, we can sink roots of identity, it seems to be just as important to maintain a global-minded openness at the same time. In my mind, there is no contradiction between being a good citizen of a nation or town and being a good citizen of the world. What we must do now is to create the circumstances where people are able to be both without friction. One's identity *vis-à-vis* the locality, the nation, and the world should never be mutually exclusive, nor should anyone ever have to choose among any of them.

Tehranian: The lives of such great leaders as Gandhi and Martin Luther King testify to the possibility of people overcoming contradictions to discover deeper identity on all levels. In Kurosawa's great films also, we witness a unique synthesis of the local and global. In the poetry of Hafez, too, images are both particular and universal. All great lives and arts share that same quality.

Ikeda: I would like to talk now about what it takes to be a global citizen. I always think of Karl Jaspers when I start talking about this subject. Hannah Arendt, who was very close to him, often noted how his philosophy seemed to have a thematic design for cosmopolitanism. In Arendt's view, it is not surprising if, when confronted by the unbearable burdens of "global responsibility", people react with political indifference, isolationist nationalism, or desperate resistance against all authority. More than any other philosopher, Jaspers understood the nature and roots of these spiritual and political realities, but that never stopped him from trying to build a philosophy that pulled toward cosmopolitanism, based on his belief in the human spirit.

Tehranian: Yet I can really appreciate Arendt's criticism of the way people in general often seem to react to global problems.

Ikeda: Jaspers was indeed unusual. There is an anecdote that I think epitomizes his greatness as a philosopher and strongly suggests the qualities a true world citizen must have in our era, too. During the second world war, Jaspers' Jewish wife Gertrude, out of her love for Germany, was harshly critical of all those Germans she saw selling out to Hitler without a murmur. But when she attacked Germany for having lost its soul, Jaspers responded, "Try to think of me as Germany" (Terawaki Hironobu, *Yasupasu jitsuzon to seiji shiso* [The Existentialist and Political Thought of Jaspers], 1991, p. 15).

He lived that belief—that people are never beyond redemption. Having a Jewish wife, Jaspers was barred from all public activities, but he was nonetheless determined to live "not as Germany trampled underfoot by fascism", but as a "model citizen" embodying the real Germany. For Jaspers, that was how he survived an era of raving insanity without losing himself.

Tehranian: That shows that being a good global citizen begins by being a good local and national citizen.

Peace Education and the Training of Young People

Ikeda: In a slightly different vein, I understand that you are interested in the United Nations University proposals regarding "global learning", and that you see a real need for the kind of education that will help people become open-minded, active world citizens.

Tehranian: That is absolutely correct. The United Nations University uses that term to express the concept of a generous, earth-sized perspective that can respond to the "global village" that our planet has become. My good friend, the late Eddie Ploman, initiated that program when he was UNU vice-rector. Global learning is a task that recognizes no limits of nationality, race, or age, but must involve everyone. We are all living in an increasingly globalized world. However, much of our education is shaped by national education systems operating within the confines of national territories and cultures. We are thus unprepared for a world that is rapidly unfolding right before our own eyes.

Our politicians still operate on the basis of outmoded concepts of national security defined in such terms as arsenals of nuclear weapons that do not recognize national boundaries. In case of a nuclear war, the greatest number of victims will be determined by which way the wind blows. Our educators wish to inculcate in our youth notions of patriotism that divide the world between "us" and "them". Our journalists publicize only the international events that attract the biggest audiences and highest ratings by stereotyping the rest of the world as bizarre, uncouth, and uncivilized.

Ikeda: Globalization may be affecting some aspects of our world, but it certainly is not having much of an impact in areas that could really influence the way people think, namely domestic politics, education, and the assumptions informing mass communications and the media. It is this gap that is most troubling.

Tehranian: I believe that the most effective method of dealing with these problems is to focus on youth. The German Green Party leader Rudolph Bahro wrote, "When the forms of an old culture are dying, the new culture is created by a few people who are not afraid to be insecure." I take that statement to say those people who are not afraid to believe, to doubt, and to learn will be there to bring in a new era. That positions the youth as pioneers of value creation.

We need to educate a new generation of humanity that has profound respect for all life and all manifestations of the human genius regardless of race, color, or creed. My own education is testimony to this need.

Ikeda: It would be very interesting to hear about your own experiences.

Tehranian: To begin with, in 1955 I had the privilege of participating in a youth forum organized by the *New York Herald Tribune*. I was part of a group of thirty-five high school seniors selected from as many countries through an essay contest. We each came to the United States to spend three months in order to live in a variety of volunteer families, attend high school with youth of our own age, give talks about our own countries and cultures, and to participate in meetings at the United Nations and elsewhere to discuss world problems and prospects for peace. That experience left an indelible mark on my mind. I became a global citizen for life.

Within a short period of time I received a crash course on American culture by living with Jewish, Protestant, Catholic, and African-American families while attending local high schools. At the same time, I also received a firsthand education on the conflicts among Indians and Pakistanis, Arabs and Israelis, and black and white South Africans.

Ikeda: That was certainly a valuable opportunity for you. To be able to get to know a lot of different kinds of people when you are young helps immensely to broaden your views. Creating such opportunities is one of the ways in which we can prepare an environment where young people, with their receptive minds and hopeful hearts, will be able to develop the courage and intelligence they will need for building peace. It is one of the primary goals of SGI's programs supporting youth around the world.

Dr. Galtung once spoke of how important human resources are, people who have both a "passionate dedication to peace and wisdom for peace". At Soka University, which was founded to be a "fortress of peace," we consider it a big part of our mission to educate young people to become the specialists and "human resources" able to help institute and maintain peace among all people. Dr. Galtung made a significant contribution to that goal by coming to the university to give a series of special lectures. Although the time was short, his talks impressed the students deeply. Later some of them told me that having heard him speak, they now wanted not to be peace researchers, but peace workers.

Tehranian: I, too, have high expectations that out of Soka University, in fulfillment of its worthy ideals, successive groups of well qualified peace workers will emerge and will make a difference in the world. In due course I hope the Toda Institute will be able to launch its own project, a program of peace education aimed at the generation who will be the leaders of tomorrow. I have already given the proposed project a name, Toda Institute Forum of Global Learning and Leadership for Youth (FLLY). The forum I envision will be held regularly and will offer participants the same opportunity I had as a youth to meet young people from other countries, exchange ideas, and broaden their horizons. In order to provide maximum global exposure, the forum could be held in a different part of the world each year.

Ikeda: During discussions with me, Dr. Galtung made the perceptive observation that the focus of peace studies is steadily moving away from knowledge-centered peace research to skill- and technique-centered peace training. I think the Toda Institute could provide an even more comprehensive program of peace education for youth around the world. Young people are our hope for the future. They have the power to make it better. That is why I am doing everything I can to contribute to their education, and why I would encourage such a program by the Toda Institute.

Perhaps the best training ground for youth is among themselves and many different sorts of people with whom they can interact, exchange ideas, and go out into the world to learn what they can do to improve it. When young people burn with the desire for peace, the fire in their hearts lights up the hearts of others until together it becomes a blazing beacon of hope that promises to rescue humankind from the darkness that has covered our world for so long.

CHAPTER 11

Choose Dialogue

Ikeda: The Toda Institute-sponsored conferences in Turkey and Cyprus were great successes, I hear.

Tehranian: The Toda conferences were the first and second meetings of the International Commission for Security and Cooperation in West Asia, held in Istanbul and Limassol in 1999 and 2000. They were followed by meetings in Doha (2001) and Limassol (2002). The Toda project was also the first NGO initiative for peace building in the Persian Gulf region. With representatives from the [eight] littoral states, the five permanent members of the UN Security Council, and others participating, the discussions were very lively and fruitful.

As you know, the Persian Gulf region has been extremely volatile, marked by high tension and entangled conflict of interests, as demonstrated by the Iran-Iraq War and the Gulf War. That is why at first I really had to rack my brains over how to steer the meeting. Fortunately, all the participants understood perfectly well the objectives of the conference—to bring about a lasting peace and economic stability in the region. As a result, the discussions proceeded quite smoothly and constructively.

Ikeda: I'm very pleased to hear that. The Persian Gulf region is a particularly crucial area for world peace. But partly because of its vast distance from Japan, we tend to have less than enough interest in what is going on there. That makes it all the more significant for a peace research center based in Tokyo to contribute positively to the peace of the region.

Tehranian: Absolutely. Nonprofit, non-governmental organizations (NGOs) must take active initiatives for peace. I see no other way to bring about a positive change in the situation. The Toda Institute focuses on "human security" in all of its research projects, which means that we seek solutions to pertinent issues from the point of view of how to protect human lives, by transcending national interests—"human security", including physical and social security.

Ikeda: That is a crucial point. How to safeguard the value of human life is going to be the central issue in considering international security in the 21st century.

It was exactly from that perspective that I gave a lecture at the East-West Center in Hawaii in 1995 on the theme of "Peace and Human Security". At the dawn of the 21st century, an increasing number of people are beginning to share an awareness of how important it is to direct serious attention to the sanctity of each and every human life. As a Buddhist, I have been saying this for years, but at long last it is becoming a major current of the times.

I suggest now that we first analyze some of the key currents in the contemporary world, and then talk about the basic orientation that the twenty-first century civilization should assume.

Tehranian: Fine. As I pointed out earlier in our discussion, the rapid globalization of our time is creating both positive and negative consequences. On the positive side, we are witnessing an unprecedented rise of global consciousness and a sense of solidarity on such issues as human rights, hunger, global warming, and the environment, as well as a ban on land mines, and on nuclear, chemical, and biological weapons.

On the negative side, globalization is dislocating the national economies by shifting industries from high to low wage, rent, tax, and government-regulation areas of the world. Domestic industries in many countries are now being exposed to severe worldwide competition. I consider the growing gaps between developed and developing countries, the so-called North and South, as the central problem of our century. That problem cannot be understood let alone solved without dialogue.

Ikeda: Relocating production sites overseas for more profit and less cost has been a notable phenomenon in Japan since the 1980s. While overseas production is necessary for the survival of industry, it has created the grave problem of "de-industrialization".

Tehranian: That is correct. While these shifts may have increased corporate profits and redistributed income in favor of the developing countries, the industrialized countries are suffering from high unemployment and the collapse of their welfare states. That, in turn, is exacerbating ethnic, religious, and class conflicts against immigrants and developing countries, and encouraging an atmosphere of xenophobia and isolationism.

Average unemployment rate is more than 10 percent in the European Union at a time when the states are losing ground in tax revenues, partly because of globalization and electronic fund transfers. A consequent decline in the state's ability to pay for welfare and social services is gradually producing various political crises, as witnessed in the rise of rightist movements in Europe and the United States. The North-South problem is thus domestic as well as international. It is widening the income gaps within and among countries.

Behind the series of economic crises that began with the collapse of Thailand's currency in July 1997 are said to be groups of speculative investments called "hedge funds". We are now in an age when huge amounts of funds can move instantaneously from one financial market to another, threatening to destroy the national economy of a country. This movement of funds larger than some national budgets is unprecedented in human history.

Ikeda: In the 1990s, many economies went down. The Russian economy was strangled by an outflow of confidence, there was the currency crisis in Brazil, and the Asian crash, all of which sent shock waves around the world. Some even feared a replay of the Great Depression triggered by the stock market crash in New York in 1929.

Even if things do not go that far, an economic crisis often sets in motion a large-scale social unrest and political turmoil; history is unambiguous on this point.

Tehranian: Very true. The Great Depression did give rise to political extremism. Totalitarian movements such as communism and fascism gained impetus from economic crises. I hope that we have learned enough from the past not to take the same road, but when people are desperate, the historical lessons of the past are rapidly forgotten.

Dangers of Further Division

Ikeda: How should we go about overcoming such tendencies so as not to repeat the same tragedies?

A little while ago, I had a chance to talk with Professor Lester Thurow, the author of *The Zero-Sum Society: Distribution and the Possibilities for Economic Change* (1981). The MIT economist and I agreed that the greater a crisis, the more we need truly competent leaders who will carry out changes with courage and fortitude. I also think it is crucial to strengthen the power of people to prevent politics from swinging toward extremism. Those awakened to the critical realities of our time must join hands to defend justice and freedom.

Tehranian: I agree with you. I would also say that we must keep a critical eye on the flaws of contemporary capitalism. The annual convention of the 1999 World Economic Forum held in Davos, Switzerland addressed the theme, "Responsible Globality: Managing the Impact of Globalization". As suggested by this theme, globalization devoid of any rules or constraints could be extremely dangerous.

Ikeda: Professor Thurow, too, was deeply concerned about such a danger. He is one economist who has repeatedly pointed out the "shortsightedness" that plagues capitalist economies where the law of the jungle prevails. Unless the world market is somehow regulated, the less competitive, weak countries are bound to become the victim of the strong, taking with them ordinary innocent men and women.

Another thing Professor Thurow sees necessary for capitalism to remain a viable economic system is the shift from the ideology of "consumption" to that of "construction". We must leave behind the "zero-sum economy" where gain for one person means loss for someone else. We must try to build a "symbiotic" economic system in which members of society share values and impart them to each other, thereby creating new values together.

To build such an economic system, we need a system of ideas that will provide it a solid philosophical foundation.

Tehranian: Professor Amartya Sen from India, the first Asian winner of the Nobel Prize in economics for 1998, starts with the basic premise of how to improve human life. From that vantage point, Professor Sen addresses himself to the questions of how people should live, what is true affluence, and what constitutes human welfare. He has also taken a new approach to the problems of development and freedom.

I find in his approach warm sympathy with human beings. It does stir a responsive chord in my mind. A society where only the strong flourish while the misery of the weak is left to intensify ends up in destroying itself.

Ikeda: Exactly. The point of departure for Professor Sen's economics is his earnest yearning to "eradicate hunger and poverty" and "fight against social injustice". As he stands by the weak in society, he has shed the light of philosophy and ethics on modern economics. Professor Sen fundamentally questions the image of human beings preoccupied with the pursuit of self-interest that mainstream economists have heretofore taken for granted. He calls people representing that image "rational fools".

Tehranian: The very fact that 1998's Nobel Prize for economics went to Professor Sen is in a sense testimony to the growing recognition worldwide of the dangers inherent in an unbridled laissez-faire economy.

That reminds me of my encounter with Professor Muhammad Yunus of Bangladesh at the University of Sydney where I went for a conference. Yunus used to teach at universities in the United States and his home country, but in 1974, when he witnessed the great famine in Bangladesh he began a movement to rescue the poorest of the poor.

Dr. Yunus soon founded a new, unique banking system known as the Grameen Bank. It provides low-interest, unsecured credit to poor rural people, mostly women, to help them start microenterprises on their own. Grameen has been extremely successful, and with an unparalleled repayment rate of 98 percent.

The method of finance Yunus invented is called microcredit, now being practiced in about sixty countries, that is enabling the poor to overcome their poverty. When I met him in Sydney, he was brimming with confidence: "The problem of poverty can definitely be solved".

Ikeda: In providing foreign aid, industrialized countries should learn from Dr. Yunus' way of thinking. Otherwise, they will continue to make the same mistakes as before. Material assistance alone won't lead to real solutions to poverty. Donor countries must be ready to share the suffering and misery of the recipient countries as they together grope for an optimum path to self-reliance.

Tehranian: Poverty and hunger will be the most serious of problems confronting humankind in the 21st century, but even under the present economic system it should be possible to solve them if we changed our pattern of thinking drastically, focusing on the human factor: how to enable people to give their best to society.

Ikeda: How to inject the human factor—the "human heart", if you will—into the capitalist economy pervaded by coolheaded principles of rationality? An increasing number of opinion leaders in the world are now beginning to realize the importance of the human factor in the economy.

Pursuing one's own happiness at the expense of others—piling up fortune atop someone else's misery—is sheer nonsense. Such an approach should not be tolerated. In the new century we must instead build a society where people seek their own prosperity while helping others to flourish as well. Mutual pursuit of mutual happiness ought to be the norm in the 21st-century society.

Members of such a society will have to be tender-hearted enough to feel someone else's pain as their own and willing to do whatever they can for the benefit of others. What might be called "global altruism" must become the universal norm.

Regional Integration

Tehranian: Regionalism, nationalism, and localism may be viewed as processes of resistance against rapid globalization. They can lead to a broadening and deepening of global democracy.

Ikeda: Regionalism has become the focus of wider attention in recent years. Globalism and regionalism may seem incompatible with each other, but I don't think that is necessarily the case.

Tehranian: Indeed. The two can be complementary, stimulating each other and thereby ensuring the sound development of both. A regional community provides a protective shield for countries and cities within the region from the negative consequences of rapid globalization.

If there should emerge an ideal regional community where member nations are tied together democratically and peacefully, while their local diversity is respected, it would serve as a valuable model for the global civil society of the future.

Ikeda: Various forms of regional integration are now being pursued in different parts of the world. Especially noteworthy is the European Union, which launched an unprecedented experiment in human history by adopting a single currency. The impact of the experiment will be far-reaching, going beyond economics to affect politics and culture.

Tehranian: True. Several regional communities have already been formed. To defend itself against US economic domination of the postwar period, Europe had to resort to the formation of the European Economic Community and later, the European Union (EU). As Europe moved toward economic integration, the United States led the way toward the formation of the North American Free Trade Area (NAFTA), which includes the United States, Canada, and Mexico.

In the meantime, developing countries in Southeast Asia and Latin America realized that their collective interests would be best served if they united economically. Next to the EU, the Association of Southeast Asian Nations (ASEAN) is the most successful example of regional integration. Among the major countries in South America a regional organization known as MERCOSUR has been formed. In addition to these, we have the OAU and OU among 53 African states, the OAS in Central and South America, and the Arab League in the Arab World.

Ikeda: A number of factors account for this global trend toward regional integration. There are, of course, many conceivable economic advantages accruing from regional unity, including more efficient distribution of resources, economies of scale, benefits of accelerated trade liberalization within the region, and reduction of costs for building and maintaining industrial infrastructure and institutions.

In a more fundamental way, many people hope that regional integration will enable member states to leave behind past antagonisms and establish lasting relationships of peace and amity.

Tehranian: I think so, too. A "non-war" system is rapidly being established in the European Union. ASEAN, too, has been instrumental since its inception in averting several regional conflicts that could have flared into wars.

Ikeda: The European Union has had to surmount a number of tough obstacles before it finally instituted the single currency, Euro. What prompted the European effort, I understand, was a strong popular commitment to peace and the firm belief that currency unification would render war impossible in Europe.

The governments of EU member states have had to transfer part of their sovereign rights, such as the right to issue currency, to the European Central Bank and the European Commission. As a result, the weight of the state has relatively declined and the walls separating intra-regional states have become lower.

Tehranian: Along with the "borderlessness" between the member states, decentralization is becoming more pronounced within each state in the EU. Cities, local areas or organizations that have common interests, are strengthening their ties, transcending the framework of the state.

Wanted: A Northeast Asian Community

Ikeda: A quick review of history shows that most wars have been fought between countries that share borders or among neighboring countries.

As you have pointed out, Dr. Tehranian, the formation of regional communities is actually functioning as a mechanism for preventing potential armed hostilities within the region. In view of such realities, I would hope more than anything for a regional community to be formed in Northeast Asia, which includes Japan, China, and the Korean peninsula.

In May 1999 I visited South Korea, where I met Dr. Choue Young Seek, founder and chancellor of Kyung Hee University. During the course of our conversation, Dr. Choue expressed his wish for the formation of a Northeast Asian Community.

Tehranian: Peace in Northeast Asia is one of the most important issues in the international community. It is exceedingly urgent to find a viable framework of solution for the issue.

Ikeda: Dr. Choue had this to say on the subject:

> Despite its long history of frequent wars, Europe now has its European Union. The region is on its way to becoming one big state. Why is it that Northeast Asia has nothing of that sort? In our own region, Japan, the Republic of Korea, and China must join hands to establish a community … .

Just imagine a situation where Japan, ROK, and China cooperate with each other, and the United States joins us as a Pacific nation, followed by Russia. Who would ever think of starting a war under the circumstances? Given such a situation, North Korea (the Democratic People's Republic of Korea), too, would see peace as their only recourse.

I have been thinking along the same lines for years, and I have made my views public on the peace of Northeast Asia. So, Dr. Choue and I agreed that our two universities—Kyung Hee and

Soka—should work together toward this historic mission for the 21st century.

Ikeda: The Korean Peninsula has been divided for half a century. But, at last, in June 2000, face-to-face meetings of top leaders of North and South Korea set historical changes in motion.

Tehranian: Since you have repeatedly advocated it, the meeting must have made you very happy.

Ikeda: Yes, it convinced me even more strongly that the age of non-disputation and of dialogue has finally arrived.

That is not to say, however, that there are no more trouble spots. Like the Korean issue, the problem of the Middle East, too, looms large in international politics. The United States has been mediating peace talks between the Israelis and the Palestinians. You are a specialist in this field. Your thoughts on the topic would be most helpful to us, especially since we Japanese tend to regard the Middle East as remote both geographically and psychologically.

Tehranian: The Arab-Israeli conflict is one of the most complex and tragic in the world. It has a long history and unfortunately is not going to go away soon. Contrary to generally accepted opinion, it is not a religious conflict; but religious fanaticism has exacerbated it.

Ikeda: This would suggest that, though it may be hard to find, a solution is possible. This in turn means that now is the time for an optimistic, practical approach.

Tehranian: Quite right. Jews and Muslims lived together peacefully in West Asia for centuries. In fact, Jews had a prominent position as scholars and administrators in the Islamic Abbasid, Ottoman, and Safavid empires. They were one of the religious groups that enjoyed considerable autonomy under Islamic rule.

Ikeda: The rise of Hitler changed everything.

Tehranian: Yes. As Jewish immigrants from Europe took refuge in the British mandate of Palestine, Arabs were displaced from their homes and farms. This was initially accomplished by outright purchases of land from Arab landlords by the Jewish Agency to provide settlements for newly arrived immigrants. But these transactions affected peasants living on the land. Before, when ownership changed hands among Arabs, peasants remained in place. When land was sold to make room for Jewish settlers, however, Arab peasants had to move off.

Ikeda: And this altered relations between Arabs and Jews. Former peaceful coexistence gave way to tense relations of the kind that are likely to breed dispute.

Tehranian: During the 1930s and 1940s, the Jewish and Arab communities became increasingly nationalistic and eager to rid themselves of the British colonial yoke. In the meantime, to secure the cooperation of both in their war efforts, the British had promised each community a homeland.

Ikeda: While the British were displaying this kind of great-power egoism, the problem became increasingly complex.

Tehranian: Yes, and in 1947, with the impending departure of the British, the United Nations voted to partition Palestine into two states, one Jewish, one Arab. In 1948, when the British had withdrawn, Israel declared its independence. Then the Arab states, which rejected the partition, attacked the new Israel.

Ikeda: The war of 1948–49 was the first in a series of four disastrous wars in the Middle East—the others in 1956, 1967, and 1973—in which many people were victimized. I was deeply concerned by these wars and exchanged various opinions on them with the former American secretary of state Henry Kissinger. As a result of the hostilities, with military and political support from the United States, Israel expanded its territory.

Tehranian: The peace process between Arabs and Israelis began to change dramatically with Egyptian president Anwar Sadat's trip to Jerusalem. In 1979, Israel and Egypt signed the so-called Camp David Accords, which provided for phased withdrawal of Israel from the Sinai Peninsula. These accords, however, left seven critical issues unresolved.

- Israeli annexation of the Golan Heights.
- Israeli occupation of the West Bank.
- Israeli unilateral declaration of Jerusalem as its capital.

- Clashes between Palestinians and new Jewish settlers on the West Bank.
- Repatriation of Palestinian refugees.
- Establishment of an independent Palestinian state on the West Bank.
- Mutual security guarantees for both Israel and Palestine.

Ikeda: Where is the key to these problems to be found?

Tehranian: The problem revolves around continuing claims of both sides to the same land. We must remember that this is not a conflict of right against wrong. It is a problem of Israeli rights against Arab rights. We need to let go of blame games and traditional notions of exclusive national sovereignty.

Ikeda: That is why leaders on both sides must have the courage to seek compromise and creative solutions. They must learn from the tragedies of the past and cooperate. Cooperation provides grounds for mutual understanding. Though members of different nations, all the involved parties share a common humanity. That is why I am hopeful and optimistic.

Tehranian: I agree. A just solution would recognize shared sovereignty over Jerusalem—a holy city to Jews, Christians, and Muslims alike. It would also allow a new Palestinian state to control the West Bank in a federal arrangement with Israel.

We must leave the details to seasoned peacemakers, wise mediators, and courageous politicians on both sides. Peace is an historical necessity. The last fifty years must be seen as an aberration from the historical norm of peaceful coexistence of Jews, Muslims, and Christians.

Ikeda: Yes, movement back to the direction of peaceful coexistence is imperative. I put great hope in the future of the youth living in the Middle East of the 21st century. The thought of Arab and Israeli young people getting to know and understand each other better inspires me with a bright vision of the future and reinforces my belief in the importance of educational exchanges.

Tehranian: I think it's a wonderful idea to start out with educational exchange. In Europe a variety of attempts are being made to foster the sense of unity as European citizens, while paying due respect to each of the diverse cultures and languages in the region. Large-scale student exchange projects, such as the "Socrates Program", are now under way.

Regional integration is significant in aspects other than the promotion of peace as well. It can be considered a stepping stone to global economic and cultural integration.

Ikeda: You're saying that successful regional integration can in turn propel a steady progress toward global solidarity and democratization, right?

Tehranian: That's right. We already have large integrated markets, including NAFTA, EU, Japan, and MERCOSUR, in that order. Now, China has outdone the United States and Japan in its economic performance during the past two decades. If that trend continues at the same pace or even slightly lower, China could become the world's largest economy in the first half of the 21st century.

Clearly these regional blocs and economic giants would have to find a way not only to coexist but also to prosper together. Otherwise, as the African proverb goes, "When elephants fight, the grass suffers". Strife among the big guys brings misery to the little guys.

The Role of WTO and an Economic System for Diversity

Ikeda: In order to carry on the work of the General Agreement on Tariffs and Trade (GATT) rounds of negotiations toward a free-trade world, at long last the World Trade Organization (WTO) was created in 1996. Now, what kind of role do you think WTO should play to establish a new international regime that would change the present "law of the jungle" type of rules and the current system clearly advantageous to only certain countries, a new system that is geared to protect the interests and honor of every country?

Tehranian: Well, we need to strengthen WTO's conflict resolution mechanisms so that rich and poor countries, big and small nations, mature and infant industries, can help each other instead of fighting to the finish. The principles of universality, transparency, and freedom from old trade relations should prevail.

As Gandhi put it, "this world has enough for all of us, but not enough for the greed of one single person". There must be room for every economy, large or small, to grow and diversify. An integrated

172

world market is not a homogenized world market. Integration is not homogenization. Integration maintains diversity in unity, while homogenization aims at uniformity. Diversity is life; uniformity is death.

Regional groupings must encourage both diversification of industries and specialization on the basis of comparative advantage. World trade should allow both diversification and specialization to grow and prosper. WTO's role is to put such an orientation on a firm track.

Ikeda: Recently we hear the phrase "mega-competition". Competition seems to be the order of the day. At this rate, though, there are bound to be countries and people who cannot keep up with the rest, are left behind in the race, and alienated in the world community. Discrimination could become structurally embedded, perpetrating a boomerang effect on other countries in the form of conflict, terrorism, and the exodus of refugees.

To prevent such a vicious circle, we will have to seek a way to ensure mutual prosperity while encouraging diversity and specialization. I agree with you on that point.

Regional blocs should in no way block the diversity of world trade; in fact, they ought to promote such a trend within and without. As you say, WTO is in a position to present a clear set of guidelines to define and stimulate "open regionalism".

Tehranian: "Open regionalism" will be an increasingly important concept from now on not only in economics but in politics and culture as well.

Ikeda: If, on the other hand, regional communities assumed an exclusionary stance *vis-à-vis* the outside areas both politically and economically, or if they became so self-centered as to intensify friction and conflict with the rest of the world, that would be putting back the clock of history.

Tehranian: A regional community-cum-fortress can become the new threat to world peace and security in the 21st century, particularly if a global economic depression occurs and countries are forced into defensive groupings. Fortress Europe vs. Fortress America vs. Fortress Asia is not a peaceful prospect.

Ikeda: How to overcome parochialism and exclusionism is the main theme of the future for regionalism. Whether the energy for regional integration can be channeled into constructive efforts for a new world order of peace and coexistence, rather than into destructive actions for division and confrontation—this will be the key factor determining the shape of the next century.

It is human beings themselves, not governments or markets, that will determine the course of history. People must be the main actors, as we have repeatedly pointed out in our discussion. "Open" dialogue and exchange among people at the citizen level will have to form the undercurrent of all international efforts for constructive change.

Freedom and Human Options

Ikeda: In concluding our dialogue on dialogue, I would like to suggest that we talk about "human potential" that opens up the future. The future does not come of its own accord. A new age arrives only when human beings are there to open the door. To me, words like "option" or "choosing" connote the willpower of people who bravely usher in the future.

The "option" I am talking about here is a forthright, categorical decision, not a preference for or a relative choice of A or B. It must be an act of choosing a particular course of action on which the person's whole existence is at stake, just as Gandhi became a "nonviolent" activist because he could not have chosen anything else.

Tehranian: I agree with you wholeheartedly. Choosing is another name for human challenge to the future; its meaning is profound and heavy.

Human beings are not totally free to do whatever they like in life. We have only marginal freedom. Our freedom is constrained by our destiny or karma (natural and social circumstances), the institutions that indirectly shape and control us (the family, schools, workplace, economy, government), and the fondness we have formed for certain relationships and activities.

Choice is the sum-total of a conscious decision-making process that maximizes our freedom by awareness of the limitations. Paradoxically, we are most free when we know of the constraints. Our freedom is maximized when we know of that which is necessary.

Ikeda: That is a very profound statement. Human beings must consciously choose their future; only in that spiritual and mental process can we be truly free. Your point is in line with a teaching in

Buddhism. One of the things Shakyamuni told his disciples before his death was: "You may become the teacher of your heart but never make your heart the teacher."

In other words, engraved in the innermost recesses of one's life is the great Law. When you abide by that law, you are truly free. Liberty and license are miles apart.

As you say, choosing is indeed a truly autonomous and most basic human act. You are not simply swayed by your surroundings, nor are you tossed about either by your small ego or by fate.

Tehranian: Traditional societies tend to believe in fatalism. By contrast, modern societies put their emphasis on human freedom. But it is clear that force, threats of force, and institutional arrangements into which we are placed or trapped, play an extremely important part in determining our behavior. The temporal world is dominated by necessity. The spiritual is the world of freedom, choice, and peace of mind.

Optimism of the Will and Pessimism of the Intellect

Ikeda: The word "choosing" reminds me of my dear friend the late Norman Cousins' book, *Human Options* (1981). One passage goes as follows:

> The most important thing I have learned is that one of the prime elements of human uniqueness is the ability to create and exercise new options and choose from among them.

I find this passage full of hope. Optimism in the good sense of the term permeates Cousins' thought, and this kind of optimism is my motto.

Tehranian: Ultimately, I believe, love, compassion, and habits of the heart ("fondness") penetrate human relations like water softens the hardest terrain.

Ikeda: Firm motivation for "human revolution" and "optimism" based on absolute confidence in humanity, combined with the "dialogue of civilizations" carried on in the spirit of such motivation and optimism—these, I believe, are what will enable humankind to free itself from the darkness of our time pervaded by nihilism.

Norman Cousins writes in *Human Options*, "The starting point for a better world is the belief that it is possible." We must begin by formulating a clear view of the world as it should be and the direction we believe the times should take.

Tehranian: Antonio Gramsci (1891–1937), the Italian Marxist thinker, once put a dual challenge before his comrades. He called for pessimism of the intellect and optimism of the will.

Your own example illustrates how to achieve this difficult combination. On the one hand, your writings never reveal easy optimism. You are always critical and realistic, some would say pessimistic, about the legacy of our 20th century of war and carnage. On the other hand, in practice, you have also demonstrated the validity of the Chinese proverb, "It is better to light one candle than to curse darkness a thousand times". You have taken personal initiatives in organizing many different activities for peace, as well as in education and culture.

Ikeda: I would like to take your kind words about myself not so much as an evaluation of my past activities as your expectation of my future actions.

I remember the series of dialogues I had with Dr. Toynbee in 1972 and 1973. With his broad perspective on human history, he dismissed conflict between capitalism and communism as insignificant compared to dialogue among religions.

He referred to dialogue between Christianity and Buddhism, but I believe he meant that the kind of "intercivilizational dialogue" we have conducted is what is most needed as humankind moves toward globalization, toward becoming one global family. When we finished our long and rich conversation, Dr. Toynbee said to me, "I hope you will carry on similar dialogues in the years to come". He entrusted to me the task of continuing the "dialogue of civilizations" with world intellectual and political leaders.

Our own dialogue may be modest, but I am convinced that it represents a step forward in the unfolding of a new history.

Tehranian: In Sufism, spiritual development is viewed as a journey. Peace is also a journey. Its destination cannot be reached quickly; the search itself is the thing. Conflict and strife have been an interminable part of human history, but we must go on without ever giving up hope.

A Journey for Peace: Links, not Chains

Ikeda: Humans are not pitiful, trifling beings simply resigned to their fate. Human life is endowed with infinite potential. We must never relinquish our endeavors to shape our own future.

Tehranian: That is the real proof of being human. At our first meeting in 1992, I discovered that we are kindred spirits. I still recall that day vividly. I remember sending you a poem the next day. Entitled "A Gift of Friendship", it goes as follows:

We met as strangers,
but we became fast, feisty friends
across the time, space,
and speech that divide us.
We forged
a bond without bondage,
a link without chains,
a union without states,
in the kingdom of the spirit.
Our language of the heart
is sweeter than
the languages of the tongue
(that tear us apart),
bringing
a joy
that unites us,
in our yearnings
for transcendence,
beyond
the finitude and fragility
of our times, our spaces,
our speeches,
and our sufferings.

Ikeda: It is a wonderful verse that beautifully sums up our dialogue.

There will always exist in this world forces that try to sever human bonds and divide people from each other. But no conflict, no strife, is ever insurmountable. We must let the force of goodness inherent in human beings contain the force of evil which is "divisiveness". Dialogue in the real sense of the term should serve as a kind of thread that ties together people of goodness in the bond of such solidarity.

Friendship, I believe, is the most beautiful and most precious jewel one can have in life. Friendship simply means being considerate of your friends, keeping your word, and doing things you promised to do. Expanding the network of friendship is to broaden the base of world peace. It may seem to be a roundabout way to peace, but in reality that is the surest, most durable path to a world without war.

Epilogue

From Professor Majid Tehranian

September 11, 2001 will be remembered as a defining moment in world history. On that dark day, terrorism proved to be a fearful weapon, deadly to open and vulnerable societies.

The root cause of terrorist violence may be found in the alienation and antagonism generated by systematic marginalization of vast segments of the world population. We now live in a global fishbowl in which extremes of lifestyles—from the extravagant to the indigent—are exposed for all to see. Global communication has outpaced global dialogue. Envy and hatred have outpaced international understanding. The enemy that emerged in the New York and Washington attacks was not a territorial state, nor was it a religion. It was the fringe elements of a much larger global resentment against marginalization.

The social psychological conditions that globalization is creating are the breeding ground for extremist politics of identity. The New World Disorder seems to be taking us into a fragmented global system. The world community must care about the fate of the marginalized and impoverished two billion human lives existing on some $2 a day.

But no one, myself included, can claim that with the eradication of poverty, violence will come to an end. None of the terrorists prominent in recent years—from Timothy McVeigh to the disciples of Osama bin Laden—have suffered from material poverty. What they exhibited is acute spiritual poverty.

The antidote to violence is love and compassion. Terrorist incidents may shock the world out of its complacency; they make us recognize the need to build global institutions for human security. We can no longer retreat into our own cocoons. The global village is here to stay with all of its promises and perils.

Where does human security begin? With recognition by all of us, born into various lives in every corner of the planet, that every human life is sacred and must be nurtured to reach its fullest potential.

Salaam & Namaste

Majid Tehranian
November 18, 2002

From Daisaku Ikeda

In the fall of 2001 the terrible events of September 11 occurred just as the Japanese edition of this dialogue was going to press. I can still feel the outrage and sorrow at the abominations that have deprived our world of so many precious and irreplaceable lives. I can only reiterate my conviction, expressed in many interviews and articles published at that time, that we are not born into this world to hate and destroy one another.

It is the function of evil to divide human beings. This world and our own lives are the stage for a ceaseless struggle between hatred and compassion. In the end, the evil over which we must triumph is the impulse toward hatred and destruction that resides within us all. We must restore and renew our faith in human goodness and in one another.

Now, more than ever, we must reach out in a further effort to understand each other and engage in genuine dialogue. Words spoken from the heart have the power to change a person's life. Warm and sincere words of encouragement can even melt the icy walls of mistrust that separate people and nations.

Toward that end, I am more determined than ever to promote dialogue between and among civilizations. I still believe—and hope that you, the reader, share my belief—that it is within our power and wisdom to free the 21st century from the flames of violence and war, to make our times an era in which all people may live in peace.

I, a Nichiren Buddhist, and Dr. Tehranian, a Sufi Muslim, have chosen the road of dialogue. We have chosen to use dialogue to recognize, learn from, and value our differences in beliefs and backgrounds, and we have chosen to see whatever differences may exist not as walls but as varying planes and angles on the scintillating diamond of global culture.

It is my prayer and conviction that the reverence for life illuminating our conversations will become the prevailing spirit of the times, and that waves of dialogue that will inspire and elevate us all with faith in humanity and in one another will engulf the whole globe.

Daisaku Ikeda
November 18, 2002

Glossary

Abbasid	an Islamic dynasty ruling for about 500 years from 750; most famous caliph was Harun al Rashid, whose court is reflected in the "Arabian Nights" stories; original capital Baghdad
Abrahamic religions	Judaism, Christianity, and Islam; religions revering Abraham, the founder of monotheism
Ahimsa	principle of non-violence espoused by Gandhi
Ahl-al-kitab	literally "People of the Book"; recipients of revelations from God to humanity relayed by prophets
Aloha	equivalent of altruistic love in Hawaiian tradition
Amin	like "amen", the endorsement of a prayer
Azan	chants, meant as calls to prayer
batin	Islamic term for inner truth
bay'a	to enter into a covenant with the Prophet and his successors
Byzantine empire	Christian empire centered on Constantinople (modern Istanbul)
caliphate	regime under the supreme rule of Muhammad's successors who took the title "caliph"
candala	a general name for outcasts, those who engage in work considered menial or

	unclean; from an Indian Brahmanic term, alternatively spelled chandala
chi	Buddhist term for fundamental misperception or ignorance
dhimmis	people of other faiths living in an Islamic community
Edo	capital of Japan during the Tokugawa shogunate
engi	Buddhist term for dependent origination, the nexus of cause that brings anything into existence
eschatology	concern with the final destiny of individuals, humanity and the cosmos
esho funi	Buddhist term for the fundamental unity of life and its environment
fana	Sufi term for nothingness; the liberation from worldly possessions and preoccupations
faqr	Sufi term for poverty, a nothingness that is the desired result of spiritual seeking
five pillars of Islam	witness, prayer, charity, fasting, and pilgrimage
Gitanjali	1912 poem written by Rabrindranath Tagore
Gosho	collected writings of the Buddhist sage Nichiren
Grameen Bank	unique banking system providing low-interest unsecured loans to rural people starting microenterprises
Gulf States	located on the Persian Gulf: Bahrain, Kuwait, Oman, Qatar, Saudi Arabia, United Arab Emirates, Iran, Iraq
Hafez	Persian poet, 1326–90
haj	pilgrimage to Mecca made once in a lifetime, for people who have the means
Hammurabi	king of first Babylonian dynasty
Hammurabi's Code	thought to be the oldest extant body of law
Hegira (Hijrah)	flight to Medina after Muhammad's persecution in Mecca, start of the Islamic calendar

hijab	item of clothing worn by Islamic women, a veil
Ibn Rushd	Aristotelian scholar and Islamic philosopher whose name was Latinized as Averroes
Ibn Sina	Aristotelian scholar and Islamic philosopher whose name was Latinized as Avicenna
Islam	literally "active submission to God"; connotes active and full participation in being and compassion for all beings
Issa	Jesus, in Arabic
Jesus	Christian savior; Islamic prophet Issa
jihad	taking to arms allowed by Muhammad only in self-defense
jihad-i-akbar	Sufi term for cleansing the soul of its impurities
jin	Buddhist term for a fundamental destructive impulse, or anger
jin	Koranic term for supernatural being; spelled "genie" in English
jita funi no raihai	Buddhist term, literally "respecting others as an inseparable part of yourself"
Kaaba	holy site in the city of Mecca
Kaku, Michio	theoretical physicist, author of *Hyperspace*
Khadija	wife of Muhammad
Koran	Islamic scripture, the sum total of Muhammad's revelations
ku	Buddhist term for non-substantiality, emptiness, potential
kupono	equivalent of the courage of convictions in Hawaiian tradition
Lotus Sutra	preeminent among Mahayana sutras, reveals true nature of the Buddha, preaches that compassion toward all is superior to personal liberation
magi	Zoroastrian wisemen
Magna Carta	1215 charter granting civil and political liberties to the people of England
Mahayana Buddhism	Buddhist teaching centered on compassion for all beings

Makiguchi, T.	author of *A Geography of Human Life* and advocate of humane competition to supplant military and economic competition
masjid	place of worship; a mosque
Masnavi	a 6-volume work by Sufi poet Rùmi, spiritual teaching and Sufi lore in the form of stories and lyric poetry; alternative spelling Mathnawi
Mecca	birthplace of Muhammad; city in western Saudi Arabia, site of the Great Mosque and the Kaaba shrine
Medina	city on the Arabian peninsula, Muhammad's refuge after his persecution in Mecca
Medina Constitution	collected agreements drawn up with Jewish and other tribes
Meiji	reign name for Japanese Emperor Mutsuhito, who ruled 1868–1912
Meiji Restoration	end of Japanese shogunate and return to rule of emperor in 1868
millet system	autonomy to religious minorities under the Ottoman Empire
mithaq	Arabic word for covenant
Moses	Jewish prophet whose Mosaic Law is contained in the Torah; Musa in Arabic
mosque	place of assembly for Islamic prayer; usually contains a minaret, assembly hall, and niche indicating Mecca's direction
Muhammad	Islamic prophet whose revelations are recorded in the Koran; founder of Islam; said to be the last of the prophets sent by God
Musa	Moses, in Arabic
Muslim	an adherent to the religion of Islam
mysticism	the acceptance of the mysterious with awe and reverence
namas kara	Sanskrit word for respectful worship, literally "I respect the divine in you"
namas te	Sanskrit word for respect, a greeting in Nepal and India

Nichiren	Buddhist sage active in Japan and advocate of the Lotus Sutra, 1222–82
nori	an edible seaweed
Orientalism	title of a book by Edward Said; a mentality of discrimination against alien cultures
People of the Book	recipients of God's word revealed through His prophets; Ahl-al-kitab in Arabic
Persian empire	at one time extending from the Mediterranean to India
Persian Gulf	arm of the Arabian Sea separating the Arabian peninsula from mainland Asia
Qureish	tribe into which Muhammad was born
rabbi	spiritual leader of a Jewish community, teacher and interpreter of written and oral law
raha	time for play and pleasure
Ramadan	lunar month of fasting
Rùmi	Sufi poet Jalal al-Din Rùmi, 1207–73
Saadi	13th century Persian poet
safaye batin	literally, "purity of intention"; the supreme test of personal actions in Sufism
saha world	this world of suffering, literally "endurance"
Said, Edward	author of *Orientalism*
Salam Alaikum	literally, "Peace be upon you"; an Islamic greeting
salat	prayers recited five times daily facing Mecca; one of the five pillars of Islam
salat	time for prayer
samgha	Buddhist term for community
Sassanid empire	dynasty ruling the Persian empire from 224–637
satrapy	provincial government in ancient Persia
satyagraha	search for truth espoused by Gandhi
Sen, Amartya	winner of 1998 Nobel prize for economics, advocate of ethical economic commitment
shahada	standing witness to Islam's truth; one of the five pillars of Islam

Shakyamuni	Indian sage; the founder of Buddhism; Shakuson in Japanese
Sharia	Islamic divine law, literally "the way to watering place"; connotes the way to salvation
shoghl	time for labor, occupation, profession
shogun	Japanese military governor under the system that ended in 1868
shoho jisso	Buddhist term for the true entity of all phenomena
siyam	fasting during the lunar month of Ramadan; one of the five pillars of Islam
Soka Gakkai	since 1937, a lay Buddhist movement based on the teachings of Nichiren and the compassionate spirit of the Lotus Sutra
Sufism	Islamic mysticism
sunna	tradition, connoting the path of life followed by generations of forebears
suq	Arabic word for "market"
sutra	literally "thread", collected teachings of the Buddha
Tagore	Bengali poet 1861–1941, author of "Gitanjali"
Talmud	body of teaching, commentary and discussion on Jewish oral law
Tariqa	"Way" of Islam, the spirit of the law
Toda Institute	founded in 1996 by Daisaku Ikeda, offices in Tokyo and Honolulu, sponsors research program on global peace and policy
Toda, Josei	Japanese entrepreneur and philosopher who inaugurated Soka Gakkai with Tsunesaburo Makiguchi in 1937
Tokugawa shogunate	Japanese military government from 1603–1867
ton	Buddhist term for greed or avarice
Torah	teachings of the Jewish religion, especially laws believed to have been received by Moses from God
ulama, ulema	Islamic learned class

umma	Islamic term for community based on a covenant between God and individuals
Ummayad	Arab empire in power from 661 after Muhammad's death until 750
Universal Declaration	statement of human rights issued by the United Nations in 1948
Upanishad	genre of Hindu texts
yang	constituent energy in the universe, the masculine
Yeshiva	institute of Jewish Talumudic learning; first Jewish academy for Talmudic research founded in Baghdad
yin	constituent energy in the universe, the feminine
Yunus, Muhammad	founder of the Grameen Bank
zahir	Islamic term for surface truth
zakat	almsgiving to the poor; one of the five pillars of Islam
Zoroaster	one of the first world prophets, as early as 6th century BCE
Zoroastrianism	religion of the followers of the Indo-Iranian prophet Zarathustra (Zoroaster)

Index